UNSTOPPABLE SUCCESS SECRETS OF TOP EARNERS

YOUR ULTIMATE ROADMAP TO NETWORK MARKETING SUCCESS

ROB SPERRY

UNSTOPPABLE
SUCCESS
SECRETS OF
TOP EARNERS

YOUR ULTIMATE ROADMAP
TO NETWORK MARKETING SUCCESS

ROB SPERRY

TGON Publishing

TGON Publishing

CONTENTS

INTRODUCTION

I'm thrilled to welcome you to this book, a unique collection of stories, insights, and strategies from some of the brightest minds in network marketing. As your host, I've had the privilege of collaborating on eight different book projects like this one, and every single time, I walk away inspired and equipped with new perspectives. This book is no different.

Think of it as a "convention in a book." Leaders from all different companies have come together here to share their best practices, personal victories, and hard-won lessons. You'll find chapters that resonate deeply with where you are right now, and others that might feel less relevant—but here's the beauty: you get to choose. Dive into the ones that speak to your journey, study them, and most importantly, implement what you learn.

Throughout the book, you'll find Coach's Notes written by me, designed to guide you, highlight key takeaways, and emphasize the insights that could be game-changing for you. These notes are my personal way of walking alongside you through this journey.

Whether you're just starting out or a seasoned professional, this book has something to offer. Enjoy the wisdom, savor the inspiration, and make the decision to apply what you learn. After all, knowledge is potential power; action is what creates results.

Enjoy the journey—you're in for something special!

Rob Sperry

FOREWORD

I'm beyond fired up to introduce this book—a powerhouse of knowledge, wisdom, and experience from some of the most successful leaders in Network Marketing. Each one of the co-authors featured here has been in the trenches, facing the struggles, navigating the highs and lows, and finding success with rock-solid and duplicatable strategies.

Network Marketing often gets a bad rap, but when done with integrity and a growth-driven mindset, it's a game-changer. This isn't just about making money (though it's a great way to do that!); it's about building real relationships and leveling up. The leaders you'll meet in these pages are living proof of what's possible, and they're giving you the roadmap to achieve the same results.

As you dive into each chapter, remember, not everything will hit you the same way right now—and that's completely alright! Some parts will speak directly to where you are today, while others might be exactly what you need six months from now. My advice? Go all-in on the chapters that fire you up and, more importantly, implement what you learn. Real transformation happens through action, not just reading!

The principles here aren't just theories; they're battle-tested strategies used by top leaders to get real, measurable results. Your journey to unstoppable success starts right here, by taking these insights and making them your own.

So get ready to learn, grow, and most importantly, APPLY. The blueprint to elevate your business and your mindset is right here—now it's up to you to use it!

John Melton

Entrepreneur, Social Media Trainer, Top 50 Earner, Network Marketing Hall of Fame

"Your drive to succeed must overcome your fear of failure!"

— Katie Anderson

KATIE ANDERSON

- Retired Law enforcement officer with a multiple 6 figure online business.

- Earned 13 all-inclusive trips in the last 6 years.

- Personally recruited over 400 people with a team of 2000+ and a 96.2% personal repeat income.

- President Club earner (most prestigious award in her company).

- In the top 1.3% of the company.

Fight-or-Flight: Managing Our Internal Response to Stress and Protecting Your Mindset in Network Marketing

Have you ever felt your heart race during a difficult conversation or your mind spinning when facing a tough decision in your business? That overwhelming sensation is your body's "fight-or-flight" response.

It's a biological reaction meant to protect you from danger, but in the world of network marketing, it can be more of an obstacle than a safeguard. In this business, how you manage this instinctive response can be the difference between pushing through challenges or giving in to them.

Today, we're going to explore how to not only manage this response but also use it to our advantage as we build our business, protect our mindset, and ultimately succeed in network marketing.

Imagine this: You're in the middle of a call with a potential customer. The conversation is going well, but suddenly, they throw a tough question your way. Immediately, your body kicks into overdrive—your palms sweat, your breath quickens, and your mind scrambles for the right answer. At that moment, you face a choice. Do you freeze and back down, letting the stress take over? Or do you take control, calm your mind, and confidently guide the conversation back on track?

Coach's Notes: Tough conversations are inevitable, but here's the key: preparation wins the day. Before every call, take a moment to breathe deeply and remind yourself that you are offering value, not just asking for a favor. This mindset shift transforms nerves into confidence. Make a list of potential objections and rehearse your responses until they feel natural. Confidence comes from knowing you're ready.

In network marketing, learning to control your internal response to stress can transform how you operate your business. You'll not only feel more in control, but you'll also build stronger connections, communicate with more clarity, and push through the discomfort that often accompanies growth.

Let's explore how we can move from that instinctive "fight-or-flight" response to a place where we actively manage stress and stay in control of our mindset.

When I first became a police officer, I quickly learned the importance of controlling my fight-or-flight response. After going through a grueling application process—written exams, physical fitness tests, psychological assessments, polygraphs, and multiple interviews—I finally got the job offer. My initial reaction to the stress of it all was asking the chief of police, "If I suck, can I quit?" It sounds funny now, but in the moment, fear tried to take over! I was scared, but my drive to succeed overpowered my fear of failure.

Once I started in the academy, I faced challenges I never could have anticipated. Training required me to unholster my gun hundreds of times a day to make sure my subconscious would work in high stress situations, memorize complex legal statutes, and undergo Krav Maga combat training—all while ensuring I had the tactical skills to survive dangerous situations and make it home to my family. The academy was relentless, but the repetition of these tasks— shooting 250 rounds a month after never touching a gun before in my life, every month for ten years—gave me the skills and mindset to stay safe. It was all about preparation, repetition, and mindset.

Coach's Notes: In network marketing, preparation and repetition build the foundation for success, just like in law enforcement. Create routines that focus on the basics: contacting new prospects, following up, and presenting your opportunity. When you're consistent, even during tough times, your business will become as instinctive as unholstering that weapon. Success is built on daily habits, not occasional effort.

This kind of stress response training carried over into my role as a crisis negotiator, where I had to stay calm in high-pressure situations, knowing that lives were on the line. What kept me centered in those moments? Repetition. Confidence. Most importantly, managing my internal response to stress.

The same principles apply to network marketing. The fight-or-flight response kicks in during difficult conversations, moments of doubt, presenting a new idea, trying to grow your team, or when you're faced with rejection. It's your mind's way of trying to protect you, but if you can manage that response, you'll see that those moments are opportunities for growth.

The fight-or-flight response is a survival mechanism designed to protect us from harm. When triggered, your brain releases a rush of adrenaline, heightening your senses and preparing your body for action. However, in modern life, this response doesn't always come in the form of physical danger; often, it's triggered by fear of rejection, failure, or stepping outside your comfort zone—things we face constantly in network marketing.

Coach's Notes: Katie is spot on! Here's a truth bomb: fear is just excitement in disguise. When you reframe fear as a signal that you're stepping into growth, it becomes a motivator rather than a deterrent. Every rejection you face in network marketing isn't a failure—it's a step closer to mastery. Write down three fears holding you back and reframe them into opportunities. Fear isn't the enemy; avoidance is.

Most people only operate at about 40% of their full capacity because the brain acts like a governor on a car, keeping you in the "safe lane" and at a safe speed! The moment things get uncomfortable, your mind tells you to stop, back off, or retreat to something more familiar. But growth doesn't happen in the comfort zone—it happens when you push through that 40% barrier.

The challenge is that most people let their fight-or-flight response control them. When the discomfort hits, they back away. In network marketing, that can look like avoiding difficult conversations, hesitating to make follow-up calls, or letting a few "no's" stop you from moving forward. Instead of leaning into the discomfort, many get stuck in a cycle of procrastination and self-doubt.

The real problem isn't the tough questions or the rejections—it's how we handle them. When we allow our internal response to stress to take over, we end up backing down, avoiding uncomfortable situations, and missing out on opportunities to grow. The fight-or-flight response can trick us into thinking we're not capable, that it's safer to stay in our comfort zone. But safety doesn't lead to success.

So, how do we manage this internal response and protect our mindset in the face of stress? Here are some tools that will help:

1. **Understand the Fight-or-Flight Response:** The first step to managing your internal stress response is understanding what's happening. Your brain is wired to avoid pain, whether that's physical or emotional. Recognize that when you feel stressed or scared, it's not a sign that something is wrong—it's simply your body preparing you for action. In network marketing, this could be the stress before a big presentation or the fear of rejection from a prospect.

2. **Repetition and Preparation:** Just like in my law enforcement training, repetition builds confidence. You need to develop a routine in your business. Whether that's making calls, doing

follow-ups, or sharing your story, the more you practice, the less stressful these tasks become. Practice your conversations, your responses to tough questions, and your mindset daily. When you know your material inside and out, your brain won't default to panic—it'll fall back on the repetition of what you've practiced.

For example, set a goal to reach out to two new contacts five days a week. That's 260 genuine conversations in a year. Imagine the confidence and growth you'll experience after that kind of repetition. The more you practice, the more natural it becomes.

3. **Time Blocking:** Stress often comes from feeling overwhelmed. Take control by time-blocking your day. When I knew I had a busy weekend of hockey tournaments with my boys, I blocked out time each morning to focus on my business. This allowed me to stay present with my family while still making progress in my work. Prioritize your business tasks, set a schedule, and stick to it.

4. **Leverage Your Support Team:** Just like in law enforcement, where we had a team of negotiators backing each other up or a whole squad of officers responding to high priority calls, in network marketing, you have a circle of influence—a support team. Don't be afraid to reach out when things feel tough. Ask for advice, share your struggles, and lean on others who have been through similar experiences.

5. **High Activity Cures All:** When in doubt, take action. I tell my team all the time, "High activity cures all." If you're feeling down or stressed, reach out and share what your company has to offer. Even if you face rejection, you're still making progress. Those small, consistent efforts will build momentum over time. And remember, it's not just about the "yes's"—it's about the effort and growth that come with each attempt.

6. **Protect Your Mindset:** Mindset is everything in business. When you feel yourself slipping into negative thoughts or doubt, remember that your mind has a tactical advantage over you—it knows your fears and insecurities. But here's the key: you can take control. Focus on your why, the reason you started this journey, post it where you can see it daily, and let that drive you through the tough moments.

Call to Action

As I look back on my time in law enforcement and my journey in network marketing, one thing stands out: The moments where I pushed through discomfort were the moments that shaped my success. The fight-or-flight response isn't something to be feared—it's something to be harnessed. It's a tool that, when understood and managed, can propel you to heights you never imagined.

So, ask yourself: Are you willing to break through that 40% barrier? Are you ready to push past the discomfort, embrace the stress, and turn it into fuel for your growth? Remember, the real magic happens when you step outside your comfort zone. Every "no" is a step closer to a "yes." Every tough conversation is an opportunity to strengthen your skills. And every time you push through discomfort, you're building a business that will stand the test of time.

You have the tools, the team, and the resilience to make it happen. Now is the time to take control of your mind, manage your response to stress, and move forward with confidence. You've got this—now go and show the world what you're made of!

"Recruiting is not about being perfect; it's about being consistent, intentional, and committed to serving others. When you lead with service, play the long game, and genuinely care about the people you connect with, you'll build a business that grows and duplicates itself. The path to success isn't always easy, but it's always worth it. Now, it's time to take action and go build the business—and the life—you've been dreaming of."

— Christina Whiteley

CHRISTINA WHITELEY

- 1200+ personally enrolled business partners.

- $100k earned within 8 months in 3 different compensation plans.

- 2024 Business Freedom Leader Award from the International Association of Top Professionals.

The Art of Recruiting Excellence: Elevating Your Game with Consistency, Communication, and Connection

Mastering the art of recruiting is one of the most rewarding and high paying skills you can develop in Network Marketing—and the best part? It's a skill that anyone, including you, can learn. What breaks my heart is seeing people count themselves out before they've even given themselves a chance. They think, "I'm not cut out for this" or "I'm not good at this." But let me tell you something: Recruiting isn't about tricking people, becoming a pushy salesperson or convincing them that you have what they need. It's about connection and sharing information. It's about serving others by offering them something that could change their lives. Once you understand this, everything shifts, because you realize all you need to do is to become a professional asker, without expectation, and eventually you will find the right people for your team.

At its core, recruiting is the highest form of service you can offer in this industry. You're helping people discover an opportunity, a solution, or a community they didn't even know existed. The challenge is getting out of your own way and realizing that you already have the skills you need to succeed. You just need to see those skills through a new lens.

Coach's Notes: Christina's perspective on recruiting is refreshing—it's not about pushing but serving. Her story of translating skills from hairstyling to network marketing proves that anyone can adapt their current abilities to this industry. Think about the skills you already use daily: listening, problem-solving, and connecting. You're more prepared than you think, and as Christina reminds us, success comes from applying those talents to help others.

Your belief and mindset are crucial—no one can deny that, but what if you didn't need to start out absolutely confident? What if you could build that belief along the way? Many of us don't begin with an unshakable faith that it will all work out, but we develop it through action, competency, and a willingness to learn. In this chapter, I'll show you that you're much closer to building your dream team than you think. I'll break down the elements of recruiting into actionable steps that will empower you to take the **daily action** necessary to recruit with excellence and, ultimately, achieve the success you deserve.

Hi, I'm Christina Whiteley. I'm a retired hairstylist and salon owner, and maybe like you, I never imagined myself as a top recruiter in the Network

Marketing space. But after eight years in this industry, I've personally enrolled over 1,200 people and built three different companies to six figures in under eight months. Now, I'm not sharing this to impress you, because starting over multiple times is definitely not something I recommend. I'm sharing this to let you know it wasn't a "magic product" or "the perfect compensation plan" that got me here. It was the daily action I took that turned into a highly successful habit.

Funny enough, most of the recruiting skills I use today, I actually learned while working behind the chair as a hairstylist. As a stylist, you learn how to build relationships quickly. You learn to listen, educate, and lead people to what's best for them. You help your network get what they want, whether it's a new haircut, a new product or a business opportunity. I built my entire salon business based on the referrals of my clients. These same principles apply to recruiting in Network Marketing. Many of you reading this already have these relationship-building skills through your current jobs or social circles; you just don't realize how powerful they are when applied to your business.

So, the first thing I want you to understand is that you don't have to reinvent the wheel. You're probably already better equipped than you realize. Now, it's about applying those natural talents to the conversations and connections you're already having—both online and offline.

We've all heard the word *consistency* thrown around a lot in this industry, and while it sounds simple, the truth is, consistency is the single biggest factor in long-term success. But here's what isn't talked about enough: *Your long-term vision and commitment to doing what is needed UNTIL you get the results you want.*

Most people fail because they treat their Network Marketing business like a sprint. They want instant results and get frustrated when things don't happen overnight. But this business isn't about quick wins. It's about playing the long game and having a clear vision for where you want to go. You wouldn't go to university for a month and expect to walk out with the knowledge of a degree, so why would you expect this result in business?

Think of it this way: Consistency without commitment to vision is like running in circles on a track. You might be putting in effort, but you're not getting anywhere. On the flip side, vision without consistency is like dreaming without doing. It's the combination of the two that creates unstoppable momentum. So, as you think about your business, I want you to ask yourself: *Where do I want to be a year from now? Five years from now? More importantly: What do I have to do daily to get there?*

Coach's Notes: Christina perfectly highlights the balance between consistency and vision. Her analogy is spot on—effort without direction gets you nowhere. Reflect on her advice: Where do you see yourself a year from now? Commit to the daily actions that align with your long-term goals. Just like Christina's journey, the magic lies in showing up every day, even when you don't feel like it.

Let's talk about the power of small daily habits. Your success won't come from a single grand gesture. It will come from the little things you do day in and day out. Consistency is about building habits that move you toward your goals, even when you don't feel like it. Here's the thing: *Anyone* can develop these habits.

Start small. **Have at least one conversation every day** with someone who could be a customer or distributor. That's it. Just one conversation a day. It might not seem like much, but over the course of a year, that's 365 conversations. How much would your business grow with 365 new connections? Now, if you want to speed things up, you can increase that to ten or twenty conversations a day. Imagine how quickly you will have results when you are consistently adding more people to your prospect list. The mistake most people make is that they reach out to people to make a sale or recruit them, but instead the focus should be adding to your list of people who will eventually buy, join or refer you. When you grow a large list, you have the luxury of having a larger pool to follow up with, as opposed to counting on a small few who may or may not follow through on their word. When you can take the pressure off of people to join you, you are less likely to be ghosted online and they will be more open to conversation in the future when it may be a better time for them. So the main goal, which is counterintuitive to making the sale, should be to build a dream team list of people you know you can help and nurture until they have enough information and are ready to make a decision that is best for them.

Your success in network marketing boils down to four key actions you need to take every day. If you do these consistently, you'll build momentum in any market, with any product, or compensation plan:

1. **Market your business.** Share what you offer with the world—whether it's a social media post, a story, or even a casual conversation in your daily life. Study your ideal target demographic; what are they looking for? What motivates them? Where can you find them? What are they struggling with right now? Learn to create content for them, instead of for you. Your content is created to constantly test the market and see what lands.

2. **Connect with new people.** Start conversations with new prospects or old connections. The goal is to get into conversations about your business naturally and organically. Asking questions and listening to find out what they need right now and what would motivate them to buy.

3. **Follow up.** Stay on top of follow-ups and nurture those relationships. Also make sure you have a system to keep track of everyone you connect with that is interested because it's easy to let people fall through the cracks. Look for opportunities to connect and relate, not just in business, but in life. The more you touch base and learn about your prospects, the easier it is to position your offer as something they need.

4. **Build long-term relationships.** Not everyone will join your team right away, and that's okay. Focus on building trust and staying connected. Even if they don't buy today, they might refer you to someone or join down the line. By acting in service, connecting people, and being a positive influence in people's lives, you can build a community of people who will consistently buy.

Here's where many people get it wrong: they focus on the sale instead of the relationship. In the early days of my Network Marketing career, I was eager. I thought if I could just get people to see what I see they would be all in. But most of the time it led to me being ghosted online and acquaintances would avoid me when they saw me in person. Why? I was trying to close too quickly. I wasn't taking the time to truly listen or understand where people were at.

The real key to recruiting isn't about convincing someone to join your business. It's about understanding their needs, their pain points, and their desires—and then positioning your product or opportunity as the thing that will help them. *Lead with service, not sales*, and watch how your results change.

Coach's Notes: Christina's story about learning to slow down and focus on people's needs is a game-changer. The shift from "selling" to "serving" builds trust and long-term relationships. Ask yourself: Are you truly listening to

your prospects? As Christina says, the best conversations feel natural, not forced. Slow down, connect, and watch how authenticity transforms your results.

One of the most important lessons I learned is to **slow down**. Take the time to ask questions. Find out what motivates people. Are they looking for financial freedom? Are they passionate about helping others? Do they crave community and connection? Once you know what drives someone, you can position your offer as the perfect solution.

And here's the mindset shift that will change the game: *Your goal isn't always to close the deal.* Sometimes, the best thing you can do is give someone the space to say "no." When you release the pressure and genuinely care about what's best for them, you build trust; and trust is the foundation for long-term relationships.

Recruiting doesn't have to be complicated. In fact, it's often the simplest conversations that lead to the biggest results. Think of it like this: If you ran into an old friend at a coffee shop, you wouldn't immediately jump into a sales pitch, right? You'd catch up, ask about their life, and share what's new with you. That's exactly how your online conversations should go.

Start by catching up. Get to know people. Connect with them. Ask about their family, their work, their dreams. Then when you hit that point in the conversation where you've gathered enough information and know why your business would benefit them, you just have to ask. You might say something like, "Hey, I've been working on something I'm really excited about. Would you be open to taking a look?" That's it. No pressure. No hard sell.

This approach works because it feels natural. You're not trying to force anything. You're simply sharing something that's been valuable to you and offering them the chance to check it out. When people feel like they're in control of the decision, they're much more likely to say yes.

Every skill in this business can be learned. No one starts out as a master recruiter. It's a process of trial and error, learning from mistakes, and continuously improving.

A growth mindset means embracing the challenges that come your way. It means recognizing that every "no" is one step closer to a "yes." It means staying open to feedback, refining your approach, and committing to personal development and skills that will grow your business.

The beauty of Network Marketing is that there's no cap on your potential. The only limit is how much you're willing to grow. So, as you go out and apply these principles, remember this: The only way you fail is if you quit. If you keep showing up, keep learning, and keep taking action, your success is inevitable.

"If you always do what you've always done, you'll always get what you've always got."

— Henry Ford

MAEGEN JOHNSON

- Promoted in 3 years to the top of the company (fastest in company history).

- Earned over 30 trips (stopped counting).

- Over half a million in personal sales with twenty four million in organization sales in five years time.

Yes Life Mentality: Being the Master of Your Own Time with Smart IPAs

Between a crying baby and raising tweens my husband and I were two ships in the night. We were living paycheck to paycheck, homeschooling, and had grouchy hotel guests with piles of laundry. It felt like heavy weights on my shoulders just barely making ends meet. No time to think, no time to breathe. Working through the chaos knowing in the not-so-distant future, life could look different. Starting direct sales and working it in the small moments of time that I had, using every minute to what felt like its fullest.

Coach's Notes: Maegen's story is a great reminder that success often starts in the smallest of moments. Her ability to turn chaos into opportunity by leveraging every available second demonstrates the power of grit and vision. If you're feeling overwhelmed, take a page from Maegen's playbook: start where you are, with what you have. Even 10 focused minutes a day can create massive momentum over time. Tune in as her story gets even better!

Then one night after treating myself to a small milestone celebration, I opened a fortune cookie at the end of my take-out meal. After cracking it open, I read the little white paper that said, "You will reach the highest level in your job." As I looked around the hotel office thinking, "Well hopefully not here," I glanced down at my laptop next to me and thought; what if I could do it with direct sales, what if I go to the top? What would that look like? But I just don't have the time. But what if I work as smartly as I can... I wonder... Where can I take this?

Imagine every day waking up with the freedom to choose how you spend your time. To say "Yes!" to the things you want to do and to shape your life in the way you choose. When you think of a "Yes! Life" your first thought is that it's saying "yes" to a European vacation, Tiffany shopping sprees, and luxury cars. While this is all true, it's not the only version of a "Yes life." The true meaning of a **Yes life** is saying yes to *time freedoms*, where you make the *choices* of what you want to say "no" to and what you GET to say **"Yes"** to.

Picture a life where your time is designed the way you choose with those activities that truly matter to you, both personally and professionally. This isn't a far-fetched "Hallmark" dream; it's a reality that can be achieved by mastering your time with strategic, **smart IPAs** *(Income Producing Activities)*.

As a mom of three, I had a toddler and two tweens. I was homeschooling while also tutoring others by day alongside working the second shift at a local hotel. I realized that if I was going to do this, I had to work *smart*.

Outside of my home, I worked most evenings checking-in guests and folding the hotel laundry. I needed to work as smart as I could in the hours that I had. In order to grow my direct sales business I was squeezing work into whatever moments of time I could find. This meant I had headphones in my ear listening to training while I was folding laundry in between guests. Then, later in the evening I could run parties and coach as the night check-in crowds slowed down.

At home, it meant major *time efficiency* and saying "no" to some things, so I could say "Yes" to other things. No more TV time, no more frivolous time, but family time and church time stayed, as they are my foundation. I just had to find where else I could pull time from for my goals. I looked at my day again and kept reevaluating until I found all the ways I could say "Yes" to work time and "no " to wasted time. I knew this was just for a *short time* and in the future the "YES" time was coming.

Questions to ask yourself:
Are you able to accomplish all of the things you want in a day? I HOPE NOT, because the reality is that no great entrepreneur can. Read that again. There is always the next thing, the next adventure, the next big goal and moment. BUT you are able to be in control of how those things lead your day. Take time to evaluate your day, then decide: Do these things help my day's goal, or do they distract me from them? What income producing activities do I need to bring in, and which activities are taking from this?

In direct sales, the challenge isn't just about building a team or closing the next sale, the true foundation is about effectively managing your *time* to ensure you're focusing on activities that drive your business forward. Smart IPAs are the essential key to this transformation. By understanding how to *prioritize* and *execute* these, you can create a balanced life where your business thrives and grows, right alongside with your personal life.

Coach's Notes: Maegen's focus on Smart IPAs (Income Producing Activities) is game-changing which I know can sound like a cliche phrase but it is. It's easy to get caught up in tasks that feel productive but don't actually move the needle. Take her advice and evaluate your daily activities. Ask yourself: "Is this task directly contributing to my goals?" If not, delegate, defer, or delete it. This mindset shift is what separates those who thrive from those who feel stuck.

Fast forward in time, I had built my business strong and I was still working at the hotel. One day while I was scraping old eggs into the trash off a dish left by a guest, I asked myself, "Why am I still here?" I was down to one day a week, and my income needs were being met three times what I needed. I was now there just as a "side security" and realized it was time to quit. I had leveled up to the next "Yes" step. I was saying "Yes" to my time and able to merge into life as a full time work-at-homeschool mom.

The key to success in network marketing and direct sales lies in working with intentional focus. By focusing on IPAs and managing your time effectively with fluid boundaries, you can achieve the balance between work and life that many dream of. This will guide you through the process of mastering your time, demonstrating how smart IPAs can transform both your professional and personal life.

Many network marketers face a common problem: Feeling overwhelmed by the myriad of tasks that seem equally urgent and important. This often leads to burnout, decreased productivity, and a lack of personal time. The challenge is not just to work harder but to work smarter—focusing on activities that have the greatest impact on your business and personal satisfaction.

1. **Identifying Smart IPAs:**

   - Start by listing all your daily tasks and categorizing them into IPAs and non-IPAs. IPAs are activities that *directly contribute* to your income, such as recruiting/prospecting, follow-ups, and presentations. *Non-IPAs* might include administrative tasks "housekeeping work tasks" or social media scrolling without IPA interactions.

   - Prioritize your IPAs and allocate dedicated time blocks to these activities. This ensures that you focus on what truly matters and minimizes the risk of getting sidetracked. Using your time and *respecting* yourself enough to respect that time by giving it your full attention. My immigrant grandmother always used to say *"Doing your best is putting your whole heart in and then just a little bit more"*.

2. **Time Blocking and Scheduling:**

   - Use a planner or digital calendar to create a detailed schedule. Block out specific times for your IPAs, personal activities, and breaks. This structure helps you stay organized and prevents tasks from overlapping.

3. **Setting Boundaries:**

   - Establish fluid boundaries between work and personal life. You can designate specific work hours and stick to them but attach flexibility to work within the wave of what's happening. When your head is down pushing to do big things your ability to be at every moment for that month might change. But understanding clearly together that also means that you can say YES to so many more things as a family. Communicating as a family is crucial, and family council times provide the perfect opportunity to discuss and prioritize the YES moments that matter most each week or month.

Years later that toddler is now eleven and has grown up in a world where she only knows her mom as a work-at-home mom, who runs on a Yes life schedule. We start our days slow with cuddles and TV time. I almost never do dishes or laundry anymore. When I go to a hotel it's as a guest checking-in ready to go on my next adventure. My daughter knows we say Yes! to things and that might mean we are choosing to say no to other things too. She also knows that mom will be there for most every sports game or activity she is in. That I no longer have to ask for time off from work and miss out on all the things her brother and older sister didn't have me there for always. She understands that sometimes mom says "Yes!" to an impromptu trip to Disney World but that also means mom might need to work extra hours in different ways. We've established rhythms, and life that allows us to say "Yes" to the moments that matter to us as members of an entrepreneurial family.

Coach's Notes: Maegen's "Yes life" isn't just about the big wins—it's about the intentional decisions she made along the way. Her story underscores the importance of aligning your time with your values. Take a moment to reflect: What are your "Yes" priorities? Design your schedule to protect those moments while staying

focused on your goals. This is how you create both a thriving business and a meaningful life.

Are you ready to take control of your time and transform your network marketing business? Start by evaluating your current time management practices and identifying your IPAs. Create a structured schedule that prioritizes these activities, set flexible committed boundaries, and watch how your productivity soars. Remember, working smart today will pave the way for a *Yes life* tomorrow—a life where your time is truly your own, and your business thrives as a result.

When the goal feels too hard we don't change our goal, we change the steps to achieve the goal. Take action now: Write down your IPAs, create your flexible committed time blocks, and commit to a schedule that balances work and personal life. Embrace the "Yes! life mentality" and unlock the potential of smart IPAs to master your time and achieve the time freedom you've always dreamed of to unlock your own version of how you envision your *Yes life* to be.

To learn more about what a typical independent sales consultant earns, visit Tupperware.com. The views and opinions expressed in this publication are solely those of the authors and do not necessarily reflect the views or opinions of Tupperware, its affiliates, or partners.

"Be fearless in the pursuit of what sets your soul on fire!"

— Jennifer Lee

JENN GLACKEN

- 30 years in the Network Marketing Industry, all with one company.

- Multiple Six-Figure Earner.

- Creator of the Social Media Champion's Blueprint.

- Featured in Hal Elrod's book "Miracle Morning for Network Marketers."

Mastering Personal Leadership and Harnessing Emotional Intelligence

Mark (*name changed to protect privacy) decided to run four marathons in a row over the course of a month. It wasn't a challenge he took lightly. While he was an avid runner, completing this goal required dedication to training, nutrition, sleep, and mindset. Mark knew he had to stay disciplined. When we talked, he never wavered in his commitment. As expected, he succeeded— and even threw in a fifth marathon as a bonus. Five marathons in five weeks. While many people struggle to finish even one marathon, Mark's discipline drove him to achieve something remarkable.

Contrast that with June* (*name changed to protect privacy), a woman in her sixties preparing for her 45th high school reunion. She envisioned herself in a beautiful, sleeveless dress with toned arms, shocking her classmates with her youthful appearance. But achieving this meant losing over twenty pounds and toning up at the gym. With only a few months until the reunion, she had a clear goal. But her actions didn't align with her vision. Her exercise was sporadic, and she indulged in bread and desserts, justifying her choices with excuses. When the reunion came, she didn't attend, embarrassed by how she looked.

What makes some people, like Mark, capable of achieving monumental goals while others, like June, fall short? Both had a clear vision of what they wanted, but the difference lay in their discipline and mindset. These two contrasting stories highlight a core principle of personal leadership: to lead others effectively, we must first master the art of leading ourselves.

Coach's Notes: Jenn's example of Mark highlights a truth we often overlook: discipline trumps motivation. Discipline is doing what needs to be done, even when emotions are screaming for comfort. Take a moment to reflect: Where in your life are you relying too heavily on motivation instead of building disciplined habits? As Jenn emphasizes, personal leadership starts with mastering the small, consistent actions that build momentum.

What in the world is personal leadership, and how do I get some?

I define personal leadership as the discipline to consistently work on your mindset, learn and practice necessary skills, stay the course despite immediate results, evaluate progress, and keep moving forward. It's about taking full responsibility for your actions, growth, and decisions.

At the heart of personal leadership is emotional intelligence. It's what enables us to hold ourselves accountable for our personal growth and actions, without letting emotions dictate our decisions. So, how do you handle your emotions? Not just when things are going well, but when you're frustrated or disappointed?

Imagine you've scored a reservation at a trendy, hard-to-book restaurant. You invite friends, feeling proud of your connections. But when you arrive, there's no record of your reservation. The restaurant is fully booked, and you won't be seated. Do you lose your temper and demand a table? Or do you stay calm, explain the mix-up to your friends, and find another place to eat?

Alex Hormozi says: "Resiliency is measured by the time it takes you to behave normally after something bad happens. With the most resilient person showing no change to begin with. Note: This doesn't mean you stop feeling bad. It just means you stop letting how you feel change how you act." This is personal leadership and emotional intelligence all wrapped up in one. We still feel all of our emotions in every situation, but we don't let them get in the way of our decision-making.

Coach's Notes: Jenn masterfully ties emotional intelligence to effective leadership. Her insights on separating feelings from actions are pure gold. Think of your own business: When was the last time you let emotions dictate a decision? Instead, try practicing what Jenn teaches—pause, evaluate, and act with clarity. This habit will not only strengthen your leadership but also build trust within your team.

When things go wrong, like a lost reservation or a team member quitting, personal leadership is the ability to push forward despite the emotions. It's about putting on your shoes for that run, even when you don't feel like it, or making that difficult phone call despite recent setbacks. Emotional intelligence is learning to separate the feeling from the action, making decisions from a place of clarity, not emotion. Learning to do this takes consistent effort and personal discipline.

Sometimes the best course of action is to step back, cool down, and clear your head. Rash decisions made in the heat of the moment can lead to regret. In network marketing, I've seen leaders make emotional choices to leave their companies, only to regret it later. It's not about never leaving, but about making decisions with a clear mind, free from the sway of emotion.

Building personal discipline to pause before reacting is key. Developing this emotional control takes time and effort, but it's an essential component of personal leadership. As we strengthen this muscle, we learn how to navigate decisions with clarity, not emotion.

Personal leadership and emotional intelligence go hand in hand. To lead others effectively, you must first learn to lead yourself. Whether in your business or personal life, you'll need to discipline yourself to reach your goals. Maybe that means setting boundaries around social media scrolling or focusing on income-producing activities before anything else.

Here are a few tips on how to better lead yourself with those specific examples:

- If you hop on social media and scroll, set a timer on your phone for ten or fifteen minutes. Go to your social account and do the income producing activities: engage, connect, post, and engage some more.

- If you don't have specific times set in your day or week to work your business, create a calendar and set times. Once again, use your cell phone to set an alarm five minutes before you start "working" and set an alarm to "stop" working. This helps you begin to work your business like a business.

In my early days of building a business, I was told it was 70% personal development and only 30% activity. At the time, it made no sense to me. I didn't want to work on myself. I tried to find customers and distributors to join my team. The reason I wasn't finding customers and distributors to join my team was because I hadn't done the work on me to learn how to ask effective questions, how to listen, how to handle objections, how to close the sale, and so much more!

When I started working on myself, the rest fell into place. My personal development journey continues to this day and I know will continue for the rest of my lifetime. Once you open yourself to growth, it's hard not to do the work.

If this resonates and you're wondering, "How do I develop this critical skill of leading myself?" It starts with committing to consistently show up as the best version of yourself. Be honest and assess your strengths and weaknesses. I recommend using a journal to do this. One page for the strengths and one for the weaknesses. The better we know ourselves, the easier it is to lead ourselves. It's not about focusing on our weaknesses and trying to improve them as much as it's understanding if we have a weakness and how to work around it to still accomplish our goals.

How to Develop and Strengthen Our Personal Leadership

Personal leadership is not a one-time decision; it's a continuous practice that requires dedication, discipline, and consistent effort. Just as muscle grows stronger with regular exercise, our ability to lead ourselves improves with intentional practice over time.

When we set a goal—whether it's in our personal life or our business—it's easy to feel motivated at the start. However, as time passes and challenges arise, maintaining that initial enthusiasm can be difficult. This is where personal leadership truly comes into play. The transformation occurs not in reaching the goal itself but on the journey we undertake to achieve it. It's about cultivating the discipline to stay the course, the resilience to overcome setbacks, and the consistency to keep moving forward, even when progress seems slow.

Let me share a personal story illustrating the power of discipline and accountability in achieving a goal. Over the past year, I committed to improving my health. My total and LDL cholesterol levels were higher than I wanted, and I knew that I needed to make some significant lifestyle changes—not just for my health, but as a demonstration to myself of personal leadership.

I set a clear goal: To lose thirty pounds and lower my cholesterol. To achieve this, I became incredibly disciplined. I tracked my food intake meticulously, ensuring that I ate a balanced diet supporting my health goals. Using an app, I tracked my macros every single day. I increased my physical activity, incorporating more walking into my daily routine and adding high-intensity workouts throughout the week. The process wasn't easy—there were days when I wanted to skip the workout or indulge in a sweet treat or unhealthy foods. But I reminded myself of my goal and the commitment I made to myself. Over time, my efforts paid off. I lost thirty pounds, and my cholesterol levels improved significantly, dropping into the "normal" range.

This journey wasn't just about losing weight; it was about proving to myself that I could achieve anything I set my mind to with the right mindset, discipline, and consistency. The same principles apply to our network marketing businesses.

The lesson here is clear: Personal leadership requires discipline, consistency, and accountability. Just like my weight loss journey, success in network marketing doesn't happen overnight. It takes time, effort, and a steadfast commitment to the goals we set for ourselves. The key is to create a plan, stick to it, and hold ourselves accountable for our progress.

But here's the challenge: Many people start with the best intentions but struggle to maintain discipline and consistency over time. They set goals but fail to follow through because life gets in the way, or they lose motivation and don't "feel" like working when results aren't immediate. This lack of follow-through is one of the biggest barriers to success in network marketing—and in life. It's letting emotions get in the way of action.

So, how can we develop and strengthen our personal leadership through discipline and accountability?

Here are three strategies:

1. **Set Clear, Achievable Goals:** Just like I did with my weight loss, start with a specific, measurable goal. Break it down into smaller, manageable steps, and set deadlines for each milestone. This makes the goal less daunting and helps you track your progress over time.

2. **Create a Plan and Stick to it:** Discipline is about doing what needs to be done, even when you don't feel like it. Follow a daily or weekly plan that outlines the actions you need to take to achieve your goal. Whether making a certain number of calls, following up with leads, or posting on social media, commit to sticking to your plan no matter what. Hopefully, your team offers a Daily Method of Operation (DMO), or you can create one for yourself!

3. **Track Your Progress and Hold Yourself Accountable:** Keep a record of your actions and progress. This could be a journal, an app, or a simple checklist. Regularly review your progress to see what's working and where you might need to adjust your approach. If you fall off track, don't be too hard on yourself—get back to it as quickly as possible. Accountability isn't about perfection; it's about persistence.

Personal leadership and emotional intelligence are the foundations of lasting achievement in network marketing. By mastering personal leadership, we guide ourselves toward growth and empower those around us to do the same.

Remember, your journey as a leader begins with you. Whether you're striving to reach a health goal or aiming to build a thriving, sustainable network marketing business, the principles of discipline, consistency, and accountability remain the same. These principles help you achieve your goals and set a powerful example for others to follow, inspiring them along the way.

Coach's Notes: Jenn's focus on discipline and accountability is a powerful call to action. Her personal story of lowering her cholesterol and losing thirty pounds illustrates what's possible when you commit fully to a goal. The same applies to your business. Write down one specific goal you've been avoiding and outline the first small step you'll take today. Remember, it's not about perfection—it's about progress.

In the end, the most successful network marketers are those who have mastered the art of leading themselves first. When you lead yourself with commitment and emotional intelligence, you model this behavior for your entire team. Your personal leadership will inspire your team and ultimately drive your business to new heights of success and fulfillment.

Take the time to invest in your personal leadership. Set your goals, create your plan, and commit to the daily actions that will bring you closer to your vision. With discipline, consistency, and emotional intelligence, there's nothing you can't achieve. Your journey to greatness starts with the decision to lead yourself well.

"The grass is not greener on the other side, the grass is greener where you water it."

– Aurthur Neil Barringham

LOUISE GATLAND

- Transformational Leader: Recognized for turning personal challenges into stepping stones for success and inspiring others to do the same.

- Six-Figure Income Earner: Achieved six-figure annual income within nine months of a mindset shift, proving the power of personal development in network marketing.

- Sought-After Speaker: Has spoken on stages across the USA and UK, sharing knowledge and experience with thousands through training, presentations, and testimonials.

- Resilient Business Builder: Successfully rebuilt and led a thriving team after overcoming significant setbacks, including the loss of half the organization during challenging times.

- Personal Development Advocate: Passionate about helping others unlock their full potential by fostering a growth mindset, self-confidence, and a positive attitude through personal development practices.

Unlocking Your Potential: The Power of Personal Development in Network Marketing

Imagine standing at a crossroads. One path leads to a life you've always known—a place filled with frustration, self-doubt, and limitations. The other path promises a life of purpose, fulfillment, and success. The only thing standing between you and that life is your mindset. Often, we don't realize that our thoughts, beliefs, and inner dialogue shape our reality. What if unlocking your potential was simply a matter of changing the way you think?

Coach's Notes: Louise's story demonstrates that the biggest obstacles we face often exist within our own minds. Her realization that mindset is the foundation for success is a pivotal lesson. Ask yourself: What beliefs are holding you back? As Louise discovered, once you shift those beliefs, the doors to your potential swing wide open. Start small—choose one limiting thought today and reframe it into an empowering one.

For years, I felt stuck, like I was spinning my wheels in network marketing and in life. I had the tools for success, but I lacked belief in myself. Confidence was something other people had, not me. Vision? That was for those who already "made it." I was just trying to survive. It wasn't until I lost my job and felt like I had let my family down that everything changed. That moment of despair became a pivotal turning point. I could either remain on the path of doubt and fear or I could fight for the life I wanted. I chose to fight.

What made the difference? It wasn't a new strategy or a breakthrough product in my network marketing business. It was personal development. The work I did on myself transformed everything.

Shifting my mindset, building confidence, and adopting a positive attitude unlocked the success I once thought was impossible.

If you feel stuck, overwhelmed, or frustrated in your business, or in life, know that the answer lies in personal development. Whether you're new to network marketing or you've been at it for years, the real journey starts with you.

Mindset: The Power of Thought

In network marketing, mindset is everything. It's the foundation of success. The right mindset helps you see beyond obstacles, stay focused on your goals, and remain persistent when things get tough. But this isn't just about positive thinking. It's about cultivating a growth mindset—a way of seeing the world where challenges become opportunities, and failures turn into stepping stones.

Coach's Notes: Louise's resilience is a masterclass in turning setbacks into growth opportunities. When half her organization dissolved, she could have walked away—but she rebuilt instead. Her story is a reminder that challenges are just stepping stones to greater success. Think about a recent setback you faced. What lesson can you take from it to improve your business or mindset? Write it down and take action on that insight.

Personal development rewires your brain, helping you view each hurdle as part of the process that strengthens you into a more capable leader.

Think about it; two people can face the same obstacle, but one sees it as a roadblock, while the other views it as a stepping stone. The difference lies in their mindset. Through personal development, you stop seeing obstacles as things that stop you, and you begin to see them as tests meant to build your strength, character, and resilience.

Before I discovered personal development, I was incredibly shy and didn't believe in myself. I thought life was meant to be hard, that success was for others, not for me. Even though I had the tools for network marketing, I couldn't make anything work because my mindset was holding me back. I was a born quitter. Anytime I doubted myself, I would give up. When someone said I wasn't good enough or things got tough, I would quit.

But losing my job hit me hard. It felt like a personal failure—not just in work, but in life. I had to make a choice: keep quitting or fight for something more. I chose to fight. I started small, focusing on personal growth—reading books, listening to empowering audio, and attending events. As my mindset shifted, so did my results.

The moment I truly realized the power of mindset was when I attended an international convention. I watched my upline, a mother like me, who had once been shy and uncomfortable with public speaking, walk across the stage as a six-figure earner. At that moment, I knew, if she could do it, I could too. That belief became the fuel for my journey, and within nine months, I achieved the same recognition—a six-figure income earner.

This experience taught me that mindset isn't just a part of success—it's the key. You can have all the tools in the world, but without the right mindset, you'll struggle. When you shift your mindset, you unlock your potential and begin to thrive in ways you never thought possible.

Overcoming Setbacks with a Growth Mindset

In network marketing, setbacks are inevitable. Without the right mindset, these challenges can feel like confirmations of failure, making you want to give up. How many times have you thought about quitting just because things got tough or others seemed more successful?

Without a strong mindset, it's easy to spiral into frustration and burnout. But when you commit to personal development, you learn to see setbacks as opportunities for growth. You reframe failure and begin to view every challenge as a chance to strengthen your resilience, sharpen your skills, and grow your leadership.

The truth is, no success story is without struggle. What sets successful people apart is their ability to push through, learn, and grow from each setback. That's what a growth mindset is all about—transforming obstacles into stepping stones.

Action Steps for Success: Your Personal Development Plan

To truly unlock your potential and achieve lasting success, personal development must be part of your daily routine. Below is a detailed action plan with clear, actionable steps you can implement immediately:

1.   **Invest Time in Personal Development Daily**
Why This Matters: Personal growth isn't a one-time event; it's a lifelong commitment. Consistently feeding your mind with empowering ideas is crucial to building and maintaining a growth-oriented mindset.

How to Implement:

- Start small: Begin with just 10-15 minutes per day. Whether it's reading a personal development book, listening to a podcast, or watching a video, make it a habit.

- Create a routine: Integrate personal development into your daily life. Listen to an audiobook while commuting, watch a motivational video during breakfast, or read a chapter before bed.

Recommended Resources:

- Books: *The Miracle Morning* by Hal Elrod, *Think and Grow Rich* by Napoleon Hill, *Atomic Habits* by James Clear.

- Videos: Watch The Secret on the Law of Attraction or inspiring TED Talks on mindset and resilience.

- Podcasts: Tune into The Ed Mylett Show or The Tony Robbins Podcast.

Overcoming Challenges: If life gets busy, set a daily reminder or block off time on your calendar for personal development. Track your progress—whether it's chapters read or hours listened—to hold yourself accountable.

2. Surround Yourself with a Growth-Minded Community

Why This Matters: The people around you influence your mindset. Surrounding yourself with positive, growth-minded individuals will push you toward your potential.

How to Implement:

- Audit your circle: Evaluate the people in your life. Are they encouraging your growth or holding you back? Start choosing your company wisely.

- Join a mastermind or group: Look for groups where personal development is a priority. Attend network marketing events, join online communities, and engage with those who share your passion for growth.

- Seek out mentors: Find a mentor who embodies the success or mindset you aspire to achieve. Mentors offer invaluable guidance and accountability.

Overcoming Challenges: If you can't find the right group or mentor locally, seek out online communities on platforms like Facebook or LinkedIn. You can also attend seminars or networking events to expand your circle.

3. Practice Gratitude Daily

Why This Matters: Gratitude shifts your focus from what's wrong to what's right. It rewires your brain to focus on abundance rather than lack, keeping you positive even in tough times.

How to Implement:

- Start a gratitude journal: Each day, write down three things you're grateful for—big or small. This practice rewires your brain to focus on the good in your life.

- Express gratitude for challenges: It may be difficult, but try to reflect on the lessons learned from challenges. A year after losing my job, I thanked my ex-boss. It was a painful experience, but it set me on a path to grow and rebuild myself.

Overcoming Challenges: On difficult days, finding things to be grateful for might feel impossible. Focus on small wins—a lesson learned, a supportive friend, or simply the opportunity to grow.

4. Use Affirmations and Visualization

Why This Matters: What you focus on expands. Using affirmations and visualization keeps your mind aligned with your goals and reinforces your belief in achieving them.

How to Implement:

- Write personalized affirmations: Start with affirmations like, "I am confident, capable, and deserving of success." Repeat these daily.

- Practice visualization: Take a few minutes each day to visualize your goals. Picture yourself achieving the rank you want, the income you desire, and the life you dream of. Focus on the feelings of success and abundance.

Overcoming Challenges: If affirmations feel awkward at first, choose one that feels aligned with where you are now and gradually build on it. Visualization might take time, but practice will strengthen your ability to envision your future success.

5. Embrace Setbacks as Growth Opportunities

Why This Matters: Success isn't achieved without setbacks. The key is learning to embrace those challenges as opportunities for growth, rather than reasons to quit.

How to Implement:

- Reframe challenges: Each time you face a setback, ask yourself, "What can I learn from this?" Write down the lesson and think about how you can apply it moving forward.

- Reflect regularly: At the end of each week, reflect on your journey. What challenges did you face? How did you grow? This practice builds resilience and helps you stay focused on your progress.

Overcoming Challenges: When facing challenges, it's natural to feel discouraged. Remind yourself that setbacks are temporary. Revisit your affirmations, lean on your support system, and keep pushing forward.

Personal Development as the Foundation of Lasting Success

Personal development is not just an option in network marketing— it's the foundation upon which lasting success is built. Without it, we remain stuck, limited by self-doubt, fear, and old beliefs. But with personal development, we unlock our potential, expand our vision, and become the leaders we're meant to be.

The journey of personal growth is never easy, but it's always worth it. You will face moments of doubt and challenge, times when quitting seems easier. But when you commit to your growth, you'll learn that each setback is a chance to become stronger and more resilient.

I faced my own storms—losing more than half my organization, watching leaders quit, and doubting my own strength. But personal development gave me the tools, the mindset, and the courage to rebuild. It's given me the strength to inspire others to do the same. Quitting is easy. Growth is hard. But those who choose growth will always stand taller and achieve more than they ever thought possible.

Success isn't about luck or timing—it's about who you become along the way. It's about transforming your mind, pushing through limits, and refusing to settle for mediocrity. Personal development is the key to that transformation.

Coach's Notes: Louise's emphasis on personal development as the foundation for success is transformative. Her journey proves that growth isn't about overnight results but about daily commitment. Take her challenge to heart: What one personal development habit can you commit to today? Whether it's journaling, affirmations, or joining a mastermind group, start now. Your future self will thank you.

So, I challenge you to step into your greatness. Push past your doubts and fears. Commit to your personal growth every day, and watch as your life and your business transform in ways you never thought possible.

Your journey starts with you. The person you become through personal development will be the greatest gift you can offer yourself—and the world.

"All our dreams can come true, if we have the courage to pursue them."

— Walt Disney

JOHN & KRISTI OAKEY

- Top 25 Power Ranker in the World.

- Member of company's Partners Council (Leadership team).

- Convention speakers.

- Parents to 6 kids.

Embrace the Suck and Soar: Turning Adversity into Action

Success isn't handed to you; it's earned through perseverance, grit, and the willingness to embrace every challenge life throws your way. If you're looking for an easy ride, you're in the wrong business. Network Marketing isn't about avoiding the storms—it's about thriving in them, and believe me, we've weathered our fair share.

Our Story: From Quiet to Chaos

I'm a retired TV news anchor with 32+ years covering news and sports in Texas and Nebraska. My wife Kristi, my high school sweetheart, runs a thriving Home Health Care business. We've faced our share of challenges with employees, schedules, and a 24/7 operation.

Just as we were on the brink of becoming empty nesters, (we had two sons in high school) life had another plan. We made the decision to foster and eventually adopt four siblings. Our house went from a calm, quiet space to full-blown chaos overnight. We had hoped to adopt just one daughter, but God had other plans. We ended up with three daughters and another son, ages 5,4,3, and 15 months!

Now, imagine trying to juggle that: Two parents, six kids, a business, and for me, a 2 a.m. wake-up call every morning to get downtown to the studio. It's a crazy ride—but it's ours, and it's one we wouldn't trade for anything.

Coach's Notes: John and Kristi's decision to embrace chaos rather than shy away from it is the epitome of leadership. Their story proves that success isn't reserved for those with perfect circumstances—it's earned by those who turn obstacles into stepping stones. Reflect on their example: What "chaos" in your life could you embrace and use as fuel for growth? Sometimes the greatest opportunities are disguised as challenges.

Finding Network Marketing: Why We Said "Yes"

Amongst all of this, we stumbled into Network Marketing. We met some corporate staff and reps on a cruise. It was their incentive trip. We had just adopted the kids and talked about tightening the budget

(Kristi did not like that idea). But after days of seeing these ladies on the dance floor, we heard and saw testimonies of the products. So, like most, we started our journey as users of the products. But within a week, we realized we could make money and help with our growing family and budget. We also loved the mission of helping others improve their health and their financial situation.

But here's a truth you need to understand right now: Life doesn't stop just because you start your business. In fact, life may throw you even more curveballs as you pursue your dreams. If you haven't faced tough moments yet, you will.

So, how do you push through? How do you keep your business going when life gets hard? How do you "embrace the suck"?

The 3 C's of Overcoming Obstacles

1. **Calm: Expect Disruptions, and Plan for Them**
One of the most important lessons we've learned is that setbacks are inevitable. There will be days when nothing goes according to plan. Instead of letting those moments knock you off course, expect them and use these action steps to navigate these setbacks with a sense of calm.

Coach's Notes: The Oakeys' focus on staying calm amidst disruptions is a lesson every entrepreneur can benefit from. Planning ahead for the inevitable bumps in the road isn't just smart—it's essential. Think about your business: Do you have contingency plans in place? Preparation paired with a calm response is the ultimate game-changer, especially when life throws unexpected curveballs.

Actionable Steps:

- *Create Contingency Plans:* Have a backup for when things go wrong. Whether it's finding extra childcare or automating parts of your business, be proactive in anticipating challenges.

- *Time Block Your Priorities:* Prioritize the non-negotiables in your day. If you know a major life event is coming (like a family obligation or health issue), block time out in advance to handle your business. Even an hour a day keeps the momentum.

- *Practice Mindful Reactions:* When something does go wrong, take a deep breath before reacting. Handling disruptions with a calm mindset allows you to make better decisions.

2. Consistent: The Power of Daily Habits

In moments of crisis, your mindset determines your outcome. If you lean into worry and negativity, setbacks will feel overwhelming. But if you adopt a "problem-solving mindset," you'll approach challenges with curiosity and determination. Success isn't about the big wins, it's about small, consistent steps—especially when life gets tough.

Actionable Steps:

- *Focus on the Process, Not Just Results:* Commit to daily tasks, no matter how small. Whether it's reaching out to one new prospect or posting once on social media, consistency compounds.

- *Positive Priming:* Begin your day by focusing on positive affirmations or in gratitude. This small ritual can shift your mindset, helping you approach challenges from a place of strength.

- *Track Your Wins and Progress:* Keep a journal of daily wins, no matter how small. On hard days, this becomes your evidence that you're making progress even when it doesn't feel like it.

3. **Collaborative: Building a Support Network**

Success isn't achieved in isolation. It's vital to surround yourself with people who share your vision. For Kristi and I, we knew that having a supportive team in our business meant everything, especially when life got busy. You don't need to know everything—train your team, empower them, and delegate tasks when necessary.

Actionable Steps:

- *Find Accountability Partners:* Whether in your business or personal life, having someone to hold you accountable keeps you motivated.

- *Leverage Your Team's Strengths:* Don't try to do everything yourself. Identify the strengths of your team members and delegate accordingly. If someone is great at social media, let them handle it while you focus on other areas.

- *Stay in Constant Communication:* Regular check-ins with your team ensure that everyone is on the same page. It also helps to keep momentum even when life throws you a curveball.

The Rollercoaster of Network Marketing

If you're in Network Marketing long enough, you will face moments of doubt. We've been there. Early in our career, our upline left the business after going through personal struggles. It was a tough blow. We felt lost and unsure about our next steps.

But here's the thing—we didn't quit.

What kept us going?

We remembered why we started. We'd had a few amazing years, won awards, trips, and built something that was changing lives. We kept going because the mission mattered more than the temporary setback.

Overcoming Major Transitions: Our Hardest Season

Then, life threw us another curveball. Our company went through three name changes, ownership shifts, and faced bankruptcy. We lost 75% of our business.

For six months, we questioned everything.

Why didn't we quit? The products were still great. The compensation plan hadn't changed. I met the new owners. I heard their stories. We made the decision to stay, and that decision changed everything. By adopting new systems and trusting the process, our business exploded. We ended up having our best year ever.

But guess what? Even during that growth, life didn't get easier. At home, our kids had their own challenges—teenage drama, sports, baggage that comes from their DNA and early years before we officially adopted them. We dealt with it all. What made the difference was our mindset—we learned to expect setbacks and react quickly, rather than letting challenges derail our progress.

Actionable Steps for Navigating Business Transitions:

- *Adapt Quickly*: The only constant is change. When your company or the field introduces new systems, don't resist. Embrace them, learn them, and pivot fast. Adaptability is key to staying ahead. This was the key moment that brought us incredible success. Old dogs can learn new tricks.

- *Revisit Your "Why"*: When you feel uncertain, go back to why you started. What's your bigger purpose? This will help you push through even when it seems like everything is falling apart.

- *Celebrate Milestones*: Big or small, celebrate progress. It reminds you of how far you've come and gives you the fuel to keep going.

Embrace the Suck—And Don't Quit

The truth is, life will get hard. That's a given. But here's something even more important: You are stronger than any challenge life can throw at you. When setbacks happen, you must remember your "why." Reconnect with the fire that got you started. Lean into the discomfort, the hard days, and keep going.

Coach's Notes: Kristi's simple yet powerful words, "Oakey's don't quit," encapsulate the resilience that drives lasting success. Take this as a challenge: When things get tough, don't just survive—thrive. Create a personal mantra that anchors you during tough times. Like the Oakeys, let it remind you of your strength and your "why" when the temptation to quit arises.

I remember a conversation with Kristi when things felt like they were falling apart. We were stressed and overwhelmed, and at one point, I blurted out, "Maybe we should just quit."

Kristi looked at me with fierce determination in her eyes and said, "Oakey's don't quit."

She was right. We couldn't quit. Not after everything we had built and the people we had inspired. So, we didn't. We refocused, recommitted, and grew our business even stronger.

Actionable Steps for Staying Committed:

- *Create a Vision Board:* Visualize your dreams. Having something tangible to look at every day can reignite your passion and help you stay focused.

- *Engage in Personal Development:* Read books, listen to podcasts, and surround yourself with positivity. The more you invest in yourself, the more resilient you become.

- *Be Adaptable:* Plans change, life happens, but quitting is not an option. Be flexible in your approach and persistent in your goals.

It's Time to Soar

Here's the bottom line: Embrace the suck. Don't quit. No matter what life throws your way, you can overcome it. Find your reason, stay committed, and let the naysayers fade away. You were made for more than mediocrity. It's time to soar.

"You can't think and act like a victim and still expect victory."

– Bill Bartmann

RICKY DURANT

- $160 Million Lifetime Team Sales.

- 7 Figure Annual Earner.

- Qualified 14 leadership retreats.

- Earned over 10 company incentive trips.

Victim or Victorious: The 5 P's of Network Marketing

Have you ever felt like you're stuck in a cycle where your network marketing efforts seem to lead nowhere? Maybe you're pouring in the hours, yet it feels like you're battling an uphill struggle, facing rejection, and doubting your path. The truth is, as a seasoned network marketing leader earning a seven figure income, a father of two daughters, and husband of twenty three years; I had to learn really fast the difference between being a victim of your circumstances and a victorious leader in network marketing. It is truly an incredible honor to lead and assist the remarkable leadership within my team that have generated over $160 Million in lifetime sales throughout the past eight years since the moment I committed to Network Marketing full time with all I had. What I have discovered is that it often hinges on mastering five critical elements: Sharing your product, building relationships, remaining persistent, finding your passion, and identifying your purpose.

Coach's Notes: Ricky's transformation from "ignorance on fire" to a leader who has empowered his team to generate over $160 million in sales is a testament to the power of mindset. If you've ever felt overwhelmed, take this to heart: The choice between being a victim or victorious is made in the moments you decide to keep moving forward, even when it's hard. Reflect on Ricky's story—what's one step you can take today to shift your mindset toward victory?

Network marketing can be a challenging journey, have you ever heard the saying "ignorance on fire" that was me, and I will proudly own it. When I first stepped into this industry, I knew nothing about how compensation plans worked, nothing about how to lead a team, nothing about how to develop leaders, nothing about personal development and probably only ten to twenty friends on social media, but what I did know without a shadow of a doubt is THIS industry could help my family leave the throws of poverty behind. I had the opportunity of a lifetime sitting in the palm of my hands to finally break the chains of generational poverty so that I could provide for my family on an entirely different level, which was MORE than simply financial gain. For years I observed my parents, my grandparents get up and go to work each morning dedicating their life to providing and surviving, but never truly seeing the passion and excitement for all of life's glorious moments. I desired more for my children, my family. I wanted all those moments and let me explain why..... In 2018 when a mass shooter entered the school building in the district where my two daughters attended, taking the lives of thirteen too soon and wounding many, it was like a switch flipped for me. It was a moment of awakening when I realized, God provided me with this beautiful family to love unconditionally, to care for, to provide for, but he never promised me forever and if I didn't get loud and proud with my messaging to impact hundreds of thousands of other families in hopes of allowing them the opportunity to have as many moments and memories as possible with their loved ones without the added stress of past due bills, financial debt interfering in every decision and moment, I was doing a disservice to others, I was guilty of making that decision for them, instead of allowing them to decide for themselves.

Something I know to be fact is Network Marketing is an industry where you can transform obstacles into stepping stones for success, and I want to take this opportunity to share what I have learned along the way, because I know if you're reading this, you can and will make a difference too. Let's first start by focusing on the five P's—Product, People, Persistence, Passion, and Purpose—you can shift from feeling overwhelmed and defeated to becoming empowered and victorious, because let's be honest not every day does everyone "feel" like sunshine and rainbows. This chapter will explore how to effectively implement each of these elements to propel your network marketing business forward.

Coach's Notes: Ricky's introduction of the five P's is so simple and yet so profound. Take a moment to assess your own approach to these areas. Are you sharing your product with authenticity? Building relationships with intention? Ricky's persistence and alignment with his purpose helped him overcome personal and professional challenges. Let his story remind you that success is built on consistent small actions in these five areas.

Let's start by introducing you to "Jane", a dedicated network marketer who felt trapped in a constant cycle of rejection and frustration. "Jane" was a passionate individual with a great product but struggled to see the results she hoped for. Every "no" from potential clients and every slow month weighed heavily on her, making her feel like a victim of circumstances beyond her control.

One day, "Jane" decided she had to make a change. She began focusing on mastering the five P's. She worked diligently to improve how she shared her product, developed deeper relationships with people, cultivated persistence, reconnected with her passion, and clarified her purpose. The transformation wasn't instantaneous, but "Jane's" commitment to these principles gradually turned her fortunes around. Her business began to grow, and she moved from feeling like a victim to becoming a victorious network marketer.

"Jane's" story highlights a fundamental point: Success in network marketing is not just about having a great product or working hard; it's about how you approach these five key areas. By embracing the five P's, you can shift from a mindset of defeat to one of victory even if it's been a slower month than what you're accustomed to, transforming your network marketing experience and achieving the success you envision.

Many network marketers struggle with common challenges such as:

- Sharing the Product: They often feel pushy or face rejection, which can lead to discouragement.

- Building Relationships: They may find it difficult to connect genuinely with others or feel they're not making the right connections, or the judgment they might face.

- Persistence: They might struggle to stay motivated during tough times or after repeated setbacks, or when life just gets tough.

- Finding Passion: They can lose sight of why they started or feel disheartened when their enthusiasm wanes.

- Identifying Purpose: They might not have a clear sense of why their work matters beyond financial gain, leading to burnout or a lack of direction.

These problems can make anyone feel like a victim of their circumstances rather than taking control and steering their own success. Now let's do a deeper dive on how to overcome these common challenges below.

1. PRODUCT: How to Share

- **Mindset Shift**: View sharing your product not as a sales pitch but as a way to offer value. Focus on how your product can solve problems or improve lives.

- **Practice and Preparation**: Develop a clear and concise message about the benefits of your product. Role-play scenarios to build confidence and reduce anxiety.

- **Authenticity**: Share your own experiences with the product. Authenticity helps build trust and makes your message more relatable.

2. PEOPLE: How to Build Relationships

- **Active Listening**: Show genuine interest in others by listening to their needs and concerns. This builds trust and rapport.

- **Follow-Up**: Consistently check in with your contacts, offering support and updates. Building relationships requires ongoing effort.

- **Networking Events:** Attend industry events and engage with potential partners. Networking face-to-face can often lead to stronger connections.

3. PERSISTENT: How to Remain

- **Set Goals:** Establish short-term and long-term goals to keep yourself focused and motivated.

- **Celebrate Small Wins:** Recognize and reward yourself for incremental progress. This keeps you motivated even when big wins seem far off.

- **Develop Resilience:** Understand that setbacks are part of the journey. Learn from them and use them to fuel your determination.

4. PASSION: How to Find

- **Reconnect with Your 'Why':** Reflect on why you started in network marketing. Reconnecting with your initial motivations can reignite your enthusiasm.

- **Seek Inspiration:** Surround yourself with positive influences and successful mentors. Their stories and energy can reignite your own passion.

- **Personal Growth:** Invest in personal development and learning. Growing as an individual can rekindle your passion for business.

5. PURPOSE: How to Identify

- **Define Your Vision**: Clarify what success means to you beyond financial gains. Whether it's helping others, creating a flexible lifestyle, or making an impact, understanding your vision helps keep you focused.

- **Align Actions with Purpose**: Ensure that your daily activities and business strategies align with your purpose. This alignment fosters a sense of fulfillment and direction.

- **Reflect Regularly**: Take time to review and adjust your goals and strategies as needed. Regular reflection helps maintain clarity and ensures you stay on track with your purpose.

As you read through the principles and solutions discussed, ask yourself: *Are you currently feeling like a victim of circumstances like "Jane" in your network marketing journey, or are you ready to step into a victorious mindset?*

Take immediate action by applying the five P's in your network marketing efforts. Start by improving how you share your product, focus on building meaningful relationships, practice persistence, reignite your passion, and clarify your purpose. Remember, the choice between being a victim or victorious is yours. Embrace these strategies and watch as you transform challenges into opportunities for success.

Coach's Notes: Ricky's journey is proof that choosing a victorious mindset, coupled with actionable steps, transforms lives. His story about finding his purpose after a life-changing tragedy shows the depth of his "why." As you reflect on this chapter, ask yourself: What's your purpose? Align your daily actions with that vision, and you'll not only overcome challenges but thrive through them.

"Don't wish it was easier, wish you were better. Don't wish for less problems, wish for more skills. Don't wish for less challenges, wish for more wisdom."

– Jim Rohn

MANDY WHITE ESKELIN

- Multiple six figure earner.

- Retired celebrity personal trainer.

- WBFF Fitness Pro and Former #3 in the world.

- Holistic Nutrition & Gut health expert.

- International speaker.

Transforming Rejection into Resilience: The Power of 'No' in Network Marketing

The Gift of Rejection

Rejection—it's the elephant in the room no one wants to talk about, especially in network marketing. But here's the truth: Rejection is not only inevitable, it's essential. In fact, rejection is the greatest teacher you'll ever have. So let me tell you this: The goal isn't to avoid rejection; the goal is to transform it into your greatest strength. Every 'No' you hear is a step toward becoming more resilient, more mentally tough, and more determined to succeed.

Coach's Notes: I have had Mandy speak at my events and she always nails it—rejection is a rite of passage, not a roadblock. If you're cringing every time you hear "No," shift your mindset. Think of each rejection as a stepping stone to mastery. Mandy's vulnerability in sharing her early struggles reminds us that even top earners start somewhere. So ask yourself: How can I turn today's "No" into tomorrow's breakthrough?

I know because I've been there. When I got started in this industry seven years ago, the rejections stung deeply, to the point I would crumble and cry. I remember the first couple of NO's, I literally came home crying to my husband Sami telling him that I must be the worst salesperson ever if my personal training clients wouldn't buy from me. I immediately began to doubt that I was capable of success in network marketing. I wore my heart on my sleeve and took everything personally, especially rejection.

I remember one of my mentors, who was like the godfather of network marketing, told me: "Mandy, you need to get rhino-thick skin!" Once I realized rejection wasn't personal, everything changed. I shifted my mindset, built mental toughness, and learned how to persevere through the hard 'No's until I found the golden 'Yes's. This chapter is about helping you make that same shift. Together, we're going to turn your rejections into fuel for your success.

The Mindset Shift: Rejection is Not Personal

Let's start by clearing up one of the biggest misconceptions in network marketing: Rejection is not personal. Whether someone says 'No' to your offer, your product, or your opportunity, it's rarely about you. It could be about timing, financial priorities, or simple disinterest. But when you internalize it, it chips away at your confidence and slows your progress.

Someone told me that the size of the leader is determined by the size of the problem that knocked them out of the game, and that included rejection. I became aware of how I reacted to rejection and started to become determined NOT to let it knock me out of my game.

This is where you need to adopt the mindset of mental separation. As Stephan and Shalee Schafeitel explain in *Master Your Mind Power*, your job is to control how you respond to external events. You can't always control what happens, but you can control your mindset. Rejection, then, becomes just another external event—not a reflection of your worth.

One of my favorite stories to share with my team...

Imagine this: You are at a restaurant and I am your waitress. You just finished dinner, and as I clear your plates I ask: "May I offer you a piece of our world famous apple pie? It's actually won awards and you've never tasted anything like it! It's best served warm with our homemade vanilla ice cream. Would you like a piece?"

You kindly answer, "No thanks."

In that moment, am I going to go to the back and cry (in the most dramatic way with hand turned up on my forehead) and say to myself: "Oh she told me no! I am terrible at this! I should just quit now!"

Or, and I going to go to the next table, and then the next table, and the next table?

Next table, right?!

So many times we make it about us when it's really not!

Keep going to the next table, and the next table until you get a yes!!

Practical Application: Next time you face rejection, take a step back and remind yourself: "This 'No' isn't about me. It's about them." Then, evaluate the situation with curiosity instead of emotion. How can you improve next time? What can you learn from this moment? By adopting this mindset, you start to see rejection as a neutral event—just part of the game.

Coach's Notes: Mandy's advice to detach emotionally from rejection is a small but shift that makes a massive difference. Here's a tip: Before every conversation, mentally rehearse hearing "No" without flinching. Picture yourself responding with grace and curiosity. As Mandy teaches, this mindset shift transforms rejection into a chance to grow instead of a reason to retreat.

Building Mental Toughness: Thriving Through Adversity

Here's the harsh truth: success in network marketing—or any field—does not come without rejection. But it's how you handle rejection that defines your path. Mental toughness is built through adversity, not in spite of it. Each 'No' you face is a training ground for resilience.

When I started, every 'No' felt like a door slamming in my face. It took me time, and a lot of tough lessons, to realize that each rejection was making me stronger. Each closed door was one step closer to finding the right one. That's how mental toughness is forged—by embracing the hard, uncomfortable moments instead of avoiding them.

As Jen Sincero says, "You are a badass: how to stop doubting your greatness and start living an awesome life." Network marketing is no different. You must embrace discomfort and stop letting the fear of rejection paralyze you. I know that might be tough to read and swallow...

Actionable Steps for Building Mental Toughness:

1. **Set Micro-Goals:** Break down your larger goals into smaller, achievable tasks. For example, focus on having three meaningful conversations today, rather than worrying about signing ten clients this week.

2. **Practice Mindfulness:** Before each call or meeting, take a moment to ground yourself. Breathe deeply and remind yourself to focus on the present interaction, not the outcome.

3. **Seek Feedback:** Don't shy away from asking for feedback after a rejection. Frame it as a learning experience: "What could I have done differently?" This turns rejection into a chance for growth.

By practicing these steps consistently, you'll find that your emotional response to rejection lessens over time, and your ability to persevere strengthens.

The Art of Perseverance: Turning 'No' into 'Yes'

If you're in network marketing, you're probably already familiar with the concept of "Go For No" from *Go For No For Network Marketers*. But are you truly living it? Are you seeing each rejection as progress, or are you still letting it get under your skin?

The '*Go For No*' philosophy is simple: Each 'No' you receive brings you closer to a 'Yes.' It's not about minimizing rejection but maximizing it. The more 'No's you collect, the closer you are to success. Every 'No' is a stepping stone, not a setback.

When I first started embracing this concept, it changed everything. Instead of fearing rejection, I started seeking it out. I made it a game: How many 'No's could I collect in a week? It didn't take long before I started getting more 'Yes's. Rejection lost its sting, and perseverance became second nature.

Exercises to Turn 'No' into 'Yes':

1. **The 'Go For No' Challenge**: Set a goal for how many rejections you'll aim for in a week. Don't focus on the 'Yes's—focus on getting as many 'No's as possible. Celebrate each rejection as progress.

2. **Rejection Reframe Exercise**: After each rejection, immediately list three potential positive outcomes. For example: "This 'No' frees up time to focus on higher-quality leads," or "This 'No' brings me closer to the right person."

By reframing rejection and adopting the 'Go For No' mindset, you begin to see that each 'No' is just another brick in the road to success.

Reframing Rejection: The Growth Mindset

It's time to stop seeing rejection as a dead end. In network marketing, every rejection holds valuable lessons, if you're willing to look for them. This is where adopting a growth mindset, as defined in *Becoming Bulletproof*, becomes crucial. People with a fixed mindset view rejection as a failure; those with a growth mindset see it as feedback.

When you view rejection through the lens of growth, it loses its power to defeat you. It becomes a tool for self-improvement. You start asking, "What can I learn from this?" instead of "Why does this always happen to me?" That shift in perspective is everything.

Exercises for Reframing Rejection:

1. **Journaling Setbacks:** Write down each rejection, not to dwell on it, but to learn from it. What went wrong? What went right? What can you adjust next time?

2. **Daily Affirmations and Visualization:** Begin each day with affirmations like, "I am resilient," and visualize yourself confidently handling rejection. This helps reprogram your mindset so you expect, accept, and overcome setbacks with grace.

Embrace the Journey

Rejection will never be easy, but it doesn't have to be painful. The truth is, rejection is part of the process—an essential one. It will mold you into the resilient, mentally tough leader you're destined to become. So the next time you hear 'No,' don't let it shut you down. Let it fire you up. Each rejection is a step forward, a chance to grow, and one step closer to the 'Yes' that will change everything.

Success in network marketing, and in life, doesn't come from avoiding rejection—it comes from learning how to turn that rejection into your greatest asset. Now, it's time to take the first step, embrace the 'No's, and get ready for your breakthrough. You've got this.

Coach's Notes: Mandy's journey highlights an essential truth: The best leaders aren't immune to rejection—they're resilient through it. The "Go For No" approach Mandy shared is brilliant. How many rejections can you aim for this week? Set a goal, track your progress, and watch your mindset—and results—transform. Now go make it happen!

"If you love what you do, you'll never work a day in your life."

— Unknown

INNA SEMI

- Elite networker & team builder Inna has built a global network of over 20,000 people across 30+ countries, earning her a place among the top 1% of networkers worldwide.

- Unstoppable Success from day one starting her journey in 2011, she launched a new project in 2017 while caring for her 7-week-old son, quickly rising to become the #1 female leader in her company.

- International speaker & industry icon as a sought-after international speaker, Inna was recognized at "The Most Powerful Woman" 2023 event, sharing insights on empowerment and growth.

- Multiple Six-Figure achiever Inna's career in network marketing has led to consistent six-figure earnings, showcasing her dedication and expertise in the industry.

How to Peacefully "Divorce" Your Network Marketing Company

Changing network marketing companies is an emotional journey, one that can feel as daunting and painful as going through a divorce. The attachment, the hopes, the dreams you had when you first joined your company – these are hard to let go of. But sometimes, despite your best efforts, you come to the realization that it's time to move on. In this chapter, I'm going to explore how to navigate that transition, why it's okay to "divorce" your company, and how to do it in a way that brings peace and sets you up for future success.

Coach's Notes: Inna's analogy is spot on. Leaving a company can feel deeply personal, but it's important to remember that change is often necessary for growth. Reflect on her insight: Are you staying because it's comfortable, or because it aligns with your goals? Sometimes the hardest decisions lead to the greatest transformations.

Changing MLM Companies is Like Going Through a Divorce

When you join a network marketing company, it often feels like entering a marriage. There's excitement, passion, and a sense of long-term commitment. Just as in marriage, you go into it with the belief and hope that this relationship will last forever. You envision a future filled with success, personal growth, and fulfillment.

However, much like marriage, not every partnership lasts. Sometimes the relationship between you and your company changes. Maybe the company's vision doesn't align with yours anymore, or perhaps the culture has shifted in a way that no longer makes you feel at home. It's difficult to accept, but just as divorce happens in marriages, it can happen in network marketing too.

This is where the comparison really starts to make sense. Leaving your MLM company can feel like betraying all the effort, time, and energy you invested. There's a sense of loss, a fear of the unknown, and the question: "Am I doing the right thing?"

The decision to leave your network marketing company is a deeply personal one, just like the decision to leave a marriage. And just like in divorce, there's a journey of transformation involved. You may start out feeling uncertain, anxious, and perhaps even guilty for wanting to make a change. But as you move forward, you begin to realize that this transition, painful as it may seem, can lead to personal growth, new opportunities, and a better fit for your future.

Transformation isn't just about changing companies; it's about shifting your mindset. You have to allow yourself to accept that it's okay to move on. You're not failing because you're leaving—you're evolving. Your goals, values, and needs may have changed since you first started, and it's essential to find a company that supports who you are now.

I chose this topic because it is deeply personal to me, and I know many individuals who struggle with unhappiness yet feel paralyzed by fear. This past year has been particularly challenging. In January, I lost my father, and in April, after seven and a half years as a top leader—the highest female position in my company—I made the difficult transition to a new project. This decision was not made lightly; I spent nearly a year contemplating it, weighing the pros and cons, and grappling with my emotions.

Coach's Notes: Inna's vulnerability here is powerful and very brave. Her story reminds us that major transitions often come from a place of reflection and self-awareness. If you're facing a similar crossroads, take her advice: Don't rush. Reflect deeply on your values and long-term goals before making a decision. Growth always requires courage.

My journey in network marketing began in 2011 during a routine presentation where I discovered the industry's potential. I fell in love with network marketing, captivated by the energy, the people, and the opportunities it offered. As a newcomer—what I fondly refer to as an "MLM virgin"—I was passionate about my first company. However, very few around me shared that enthusiasm. Navigating the early stages of my career was tough, but after three years, I emerged as one of the top leaders in my country. Unfortunately, my first company eventually went out of business, leaving me disillusioned.

That experience was heartbreaking; it felt as though I had been betrayed. My initial excitement turned to disappointment, and I began to question whether network marketing truly worked. My views became unprofessional and overly emotional, leading me to step away from the business for a time.

Three years later, after becoming a mother, I found myself reassessing my life. I am a passionate individual who loves to work and create; simply staying home on maternity leave was not an option for me. During this period of reflection, I discovered a new company that reignited my passion. This time, I approached it with a professional mindset. In 2017, with a seven-week-old baby, I embarked on a new business venture in an entirely different market. It was challenging, with no tools, no language support, and no products initially available. Nevertheless, we persevered, and after six years, I achieved the number one female position in the world.

However, as I ascended to new heights, I began to encounter significant issues. The higher I climbed, the more I realized that the company was not willing to take the necessary steps for international growth. While I am immensely grateful for the experiences and lessons learned from my previous companies, I found myself feeling stagnant. My passion and love for the business began to fade, and it became evident that if I wanted to be happy and continue to succeed, I needed to embrace change.

In this chapter, I will explore the emotional turmoil many experience during this process, the challenges I faced, and how to navigate the complexities of leaving a network marketing company. My journey was fraught with misunderstandings, hostility, threats, blame, and personal disappointment. As a full-time network marketer, the decision to leave a seemingly stable environment for the unknown was daunting. Yet, six months have passed since that pivotal decision, and I am incredibly grateful that I made the leap.

Now, I recognize the importance of confronting reality and being open to the possibilities that change can bring. This is why I chose to address this controversial topic—to support anyone who may find themselves in a similar situation. If your desire for change is genuine, then it's time to take that step. Embrace the uncertainty, and trust that the right path will reveal itself.

The point is simple: Leaving your network marketing company doesn't mean you're giving up or failing. It means you're recognizing when something no longer serves you and making a conscious decision to find a better fit. Just like a divorce, this decision is never easy, but staying in a situation that no longer aligns with who you are will only hold you back from the success and happiness you deserve.

One of the biggest problems people face when considering leaving their company is fear. Fear of failure, fear of judgment, fear of the unknown. When you're deeply invested in something, it's incredibly hard to walk away, even when it's no longer serving you. You might worry about what your team will think, how your finances will be affected, or whether you'll find another opportunity that feels like home.

There's also the emotional weight that comes with the decision. You've built relationships, you've invested time, energy, and money, and now you're contemplating leaving all of that behind. It's natural to feel torn, unsure, and even guilty.

Another common issue is external pressure. Maybe someone is offering you a "better deal" or a new opportunity, but you're not sure if it's right for you. In both marriages and network marketing, it's crucial to make decisions based on your own values and desires—not because someone else is pushing you in a direction you're not ready to go.

To navigate the "divorce" from your network marketing company and come out stronger, there are several things you can do:

1. **Evaluate Your Situation Objectively**: Before making any decisions, take a step back and assess your current situation. Are you truly unhappy with the company, or are there external factors at play that could be resolved? Is your dissatisfaction temporary, or is it a sign that it's time to move on?

2. **Don't Make Hasty Decisions**: Just like in a marriage, you don't want to rush into a divorce without trying to fix things first. Have you explored all the options within your company to see if there's room for improvement? Talk to your upline or leadership about your concerns and see if anything can be done to address them.

3. **Make the Decision for YOU**: Don't leave your company just because someone else made you a better offer. While it's tempting to jump ship for a shiny new opportunity, make sure the decision is based on your long-term goals and personal values. Your happiness and success should be the driving factors.

4. **Prepare for the Transition**: Leaving a company can come with financial, emotional, and logistical challenges. Make sure you have a solid plan in place before you leave. This includes having a clear idea of where you're going next, how you'll handle the transition with your team, and how you'll manage any financial gaps.

5. **Leave on Good Terms:** Just because you're leaving doesn't mean you should burn bridges. Be respectful, communicate openly with your team, and ensure that you part ways on good terms. You never know when those relationships might come back into play down the road.

The process of leaving your network marketing company doesn't have to be messy or filled with regret. It's about recognizing when a relationship no longer serves you and having the courage to move on to something better. Much like a divorce, it's about growth, self-awareness, and making decisions that align with your future.

If you've been feeling stuck, frustrated, or unsure about your place in your current company, now is the time to evaluate your situation honestly. Are you staying out of fear or loyalty, or because it's truly the right fit for you? Only you can answer that question.

Remember, this is your journey, and you deserve to be in a place that aligns with who you are and what you want to achieve. Don't be afraid to take the leap—there's a whole world of opportunities waiting for you on the other side. Take control of your future and find the company that will help you thrive, both personally and professionally.

In closing, I want to emphasize the importance of being sensitive to the feelings of those in our teams as leaders. We must recognize that we do not own anyone; relationships in network marketing are built on mutual respect and shared goals. While we invest significant time and resources into our teams, it's essential to understand that if someone chooses to leave, they are exercising their right to pursue new opportunities.

For those seeking change and feeling unfulfilled in their current situations, remember that your present circumstances are the result of your past decisions. If you've decided to transition, do so gracefully and with gratitude. Thank those who have contributed to your journey, rather than blaming or harboring resentment toward the experiences that brought you to this point. Every step you've taken has shaped your path.

Coach's Notes: Inna's call for grace and gratitude is an important reminder. How you leave reflects who you are. As you make changes, focus on maintaining relationships and honoring the journey that brought you here. Integrity in transitions builds trust and strengthens your personal brand.

To the company owners reading this, it's crucial to recognize that you do not own your team members. Our network marketing business is often cyclical; it's not a forever commitment, much like the marriages we hope will last a lifetime. The reality is that the divorce rate is high, and the stability of our market can be unpredictable. It's vital to allow people to leave with dignity, offering them the respect and acknowledgment they deserve for their contributions.

When a partnership falters, the responsibility lies with both parties. Just as in a marriage, there are often faults on both sides. No one is entirely to blame; both partners have chosen one another and must navigate the consequences of their decisions together. Similarly, if someone departs from your company, they are exercising their agency, but the organization must also reflect on its practices. Companies that treat their people well and foster a positive environment tend to retain their talent.

As we navigate this complex profession, we face criticism from the outside world. It's imperative that we maintain the integrity and strength of our industry. People will inevitably move between companies, just as relationships sometimes fail. However, how we handle these transitions defines our professionalism and reputation.

Always remember, your name is your brand, and it travels with you wherever you go. Conduct yourself responsibly, make decisions that reflect your values, and approach each situation with sincerity and thoughtfulness.

Wishing you all the best on your journeys,

Inna Semi

"According to most studies, people's number one fear is public speaking. Number two is death. Death is number two. Does that sound right? This means the average person, if you go to a funeral, you're better off in the casket, than doing the eulogy."

– Jerry Seinfeld

TARA PAGE TRUAX

- #1 International Best Selling Author.

- Over $120 Million in sales.

- Multiple 7 figure earner.

- Trained and spoke on stages globally.

Wait, I Have To Talk To People?

I am not special. I am a small town raised, artistically introverted, empathic spirit, that cried if my mom asked me to order pizza as a child. If you would have told me back then that I would talk to people for a living, that little girl would have laughed in your face. Avoiding speaking at all costs was a mission. So much so that I used dance to express myself, and became so effective at it I made a career traveling the world as a professional dancer. On paper and in pictures my life looked like a dream, but my bank account disagreed, and after having my first child on the autism spectrum, I found myself in my thirties with over six figures of credit card debt from medical bills alone. It was the network marketing industry that brought me out of the dance studio and helped us offset the six figures of debt and create multiple seven figures of income. I was able to transform my debilitating fear of public speaking into creating millions of dollars building a global business, and successfully doing it all without peeing my pants, falling off the stage, or embarrassing myself publicly. I am confident, if I can overcome such a paralyzing fear, and turn it into one of my greatest gifts, it is possible you can do exactly the same through some simple steps, applied action and dedicated practice. So, let's get started!

Coach's Notes: Tara's vulnerability here is amazing. Most are scared to share their struggles but it is the most important way to connect with others. Her journey highlights that even those with the greatest fears can transform them into incredible strengths. Reflect on her story: What fear is holding you back right now? Could it become the very skill that defines your success in network marketing?

How Do You Do It?

First I want you to think of an experience where you worked hard for something and had massive success.

For me, that time was my years as a professional dancer. Not only do I have a BFA in Dance, which was four years of intensive study, I had sixteen years training before college and my extensive professional career after college that gave me perspective, built character and was where I learned real life skills, which included dedication, determination, discipline, preparation and practice. Every one of you has real life applied knowledge and success, which can be from any area or profession. Write one success down, and the skills you learned from it.

Next, think about a time you stepped out of your comfort zone. Get a clear picture in your mind. Feel the feeling of what you experienced. Write it down. Was it good? Was it bad? What happened? Did you die?

Asking that question alone is gold, as you could not be reading these words right now if you died! Dead people are not our target audience anyway. Last time I checked, building a team in network marketing works better with real life living and breathing humans, and we need to talk to them to make money. My goal is every one of you has confidence giving that eulogy Jerry Seinfeld talks about, and none of us bury our gifts in the ground.

One of my many uncomfortable experiences was at a Network Marketing event in Utah where instead of sharing my testimony, I said my name and froze. The words would not come out. The mic rolled out of my hands as I ran off to avoid any further humiliation. It was through this setback that I knew I needed to grow my skills. But here is the most important part of that day. I, like you, did not die. Which means we are winning, and that there is hope for us, our words and our voices too!

Now that we have proof that we can do hard things, let's move on to the skills.

The Breath

"See that line on the stage? Never go behind it. When you lean forward, inhale, and exhale when you lean back." This is the ONLY coaching I was ever given for public speaking in my entire career. Minutes later I was on stage in front of a couple thousand people for my very first keynote. Only one month after the debacle where I dropped the mic and ran, but this time a fire ignited within my voice.

When I was given the advice on where to breathe, I instantly shifted from concerned with the words I was planning to say, to dropping out of my head, and into my body. This brought me into the present moment.

Coach's Notes: Tara's advice about breathwork is a massive help. If you've ever struggled with public speaking or even a simple team call, start with this: Focus on your breath, not perfection. Practice being present and grounded—it's the foundation for connecting with any audience.

Try it. Breathe in right now into your belly. Where does your awareness shift? The more present we are in our body, the easier it is to connect to our audience, whether it is a Facebook live, TikTok, in-person event, team training or large audience keynote. When we breathe, it steadies our pace, prevents shortness of breath, connects to emotion, and makes our message more impactful. It also allows us to engage in real time interactions with our audience, so we are speaking in conversation with them, versus spewing information at them.

Read a sentence out loud, and notice the impact if you breathe in different places. Also notice your body language. Try five different places to breathe. Notice how it changes your message. Notice what feels natural. Notice what feels comfortable.

Breathing also improves the sound and tone of our voice, especially if breathing deep into the belly. And getting full breaths while speaking can create power and dynamic.

Now on the flip side, one of the biggest mistakes people make when speaking is they try to calm their nervous system and take too many deep breaths. The truth is that "anxious energy" and "excitement energy," feel the same in the body. We want that excitement channeled through our words, so we can connect with those listening, not put them to sleep! So make sure to breathe to center yourself, then use that energy to connect to our audience. Smiling can help with this too.

Coach's Notes: The idea that anxious energy and excitement feel the same is a game-changing insight. Instead of trying to erase the nervousness, Tara shows us how to channel it into authentic, impactful communication. Next time you're speaking, don't aim for perfection—focus on connection. Your energy and presence are what people truly resonate with.

Even after years of speaking in front of thousands and in multiple languages with translators, I still get present in my body by breathing deep into my belly and then my chest and then exhaling at least ten times to eliminate distractions before speaking. The more present I am, the clearer I am with my message. I can trust that the words that come out of my mouth will impact at least one heart in that room.

Which brings me to the next skill.

You Will Never Speak To Everyone, So Stop Trying! Connect One Heart At A Time!

Look around. There are people all over the place that we don't want to invite to dinner, we don't want to vacation with or that we can't stand what they post on social media. Yet we get upset when those people don't like what we have to say, or don't want to work with us! This is good news. It's called diversity! Our message is not for them, just like they are not for us. That doesn't mean you said something wrong.

But what if they don't like me? What if I say the wrong thing? What if I sound stupid? What if I sound desperate? What if they think I'm trying to make money off them? What if... (you fill in the blank), because I promise we have all had those thoughts at some point in our life, especially if you are a recovering people pleaser, like myself. So let's be real, what if they don't like you?

Well, there are people who judge you and don't like you when you're broke, right? There are people who don't like you when you're wealthy or having success, too. The truth is people are not going to like you regardless. So why not unapologetically build a legacy for your family so you can overflow into the world and serve others... one conversation at a time!

Find people. Talk to them. That's your job. That's it. If someone doesn't want to listen, move on! But don't stop talking to people! Ask people questions. Connect to how they can offset an ever-rising inflation-filled world with income that could help their family, and show them how they can do that with your words and actions.

Don't Read Your Words!

Having notes, key phrases or concepts as bullet points that keep you on track when presenting is absolutely okay! It prevents us from rambling. But DO NOT read your notes word for word or you will fall flat. It is obvious to those listening when you are reading a script and you will miss connecting to your audience. This is why I record myself speaking and listen to it back, so the stories become second nature. Land the message without unnecessary detail. Know why you are speaking. Is it to connect, communicate, create or to educate? Knowing the purpose helps keep you on track and adds value to your words.

No one wants to see polished and perfect, because humans are a beautiful imperfect mess. In fact, I make fun of myself often onstage. I mix up words, I say things that don't make sense, I've almost tripped and fell. I'm a real person! I point out my flaws so that all the other real people in the room can relate as well. It is our obsession with being perfect that prevents us from connecting. The key to building trust within sales and leadership is connection. So be real. If you make a mistake, make a joke out of it. Your mess is your message.

By being brave enough to create that space for others, it gives them space to feel supported and safe in learning, making mistakes, and growing from them.

Lastly, please rehearse. Professionals practice by doing, over and over. Take notes. Make adjustments. But don't over-rehearse. You want to be able to engage with the audience in real time and in real life. Remember, we want people to do what we do. So make it look doable. But don't be afraid to suck, we all start somewhere. Practice to be present. Don't practice to be perfect.

What Is The Worst That Can Happen? (Just a Hint, No One Died)

For some of us, the worst thing that can happen when we speak publicly is we freeze, say the wrong thing, mess up, or embarrass ourselves. Which I can agree are pretty awful having experienced many of those things myself. But nothing compared to the experience I had after I shared my voice. From people I trusted.

Through the diverse journey of network marketing, I've met people that have become some of my best friends and some who have turned out to be my worst enemies. Keynote speeches where I have shared intimate stories of my family have been weaponized for other people's personal gain. I have had to file cease and desists on people who I thought were my closest friends. I've done Facebook lives that I would eventually delete and others that have gone viral. But through it all I did not stop speaking, why? Because it's part of my purpose. It's all part of the journey. The successes and failures have all shown me how powerful my authentic message can be. I'm living proof of how words inspired from the heart, with action taken behind them, can propel massive success. Success that if I can find within myself, you can too.

So Where Do You Start?

Start now. Start with a Facebook or IG live, or host a Zoom. Invite a couple of friends over and share your product or services. Raise your hand. Speak at a networking event or share your testimony on a team call. Do the actual networking part of network marketing. Just start. From there the future is unlimited.

So, let's do this thing! The world is your stage. Your message is unique and placed in your heart for a reason. The greatest gift you have happens in the present moment, in the room where you are speaking. Be there. Breathe. Be in the moment and experience the magic happening as you show up with your authentic voice and make an impact.

Remember sometimes our greatest gifts are locked inside our greatest fears. Don't let them stay prisoner there! Call and order the pizza of life with all the toppings and then share a slice with the world. There are over 8 million people on this planet, now let's go find them and talk to them! Chances are you won't die, but you sure may get wealthy along the way.

"There are two kinds of people: Those who think they can, and those who think they can't, and they're both right."

— Henry Ford

LEAH MELQUIST

- 11 years in the NWM industry.

- 7 figure earner.

- 5 back to back years of multiple six-figures Top 1% of company.

- Earned 18 paid all inclusive trips.

- Currently leading a team of over 2,400 with a 96% re-order rate.

Building Unshakable Belief: The Foundation for Success in Network Marketing

Building Your Belief Foundation

When you believe in yourself and your vision, taking consistent action becomes natural. As each action builds your belief, you create a powerful cycle that drives you forward. Yet, many find themselves stuck when belief wanes, unmotivated to stay consistent when results seem slow. This chapter reveals how to break the cycle of doubt and unlock your potential by cultivating belief, protecting your confidence, and establishing routines that foster success. Success doesn't happen by chance; it comes from consistency in your daily actions, environment, and mentors who guide you forward, no matter the challenges. Let's first discuss how to build your foundation of belief.

Coach's Notes: Leah's insight on belief as the foundation for success is invaluable. Without belief, even the best strategies fall flat. Think of belief as the root system of a tree—strong roots provide stability and allow growth to flourish above ground. What small steps can you take today to strengthen your belief in your abilities and goals?

#1 - Recognize and Celebrate Small Wins
Start by focusing on small, achievable tasks. When you complete them, you get a psychological boost that builds your belief. The more you prove to yourself that you can do something—even small things—the more your belief in your capabilities grows. These "small wins" might look like:

- Setting and hitting daily prospecting goals (e.g., talking to 3 new prospects per day).

- Completing a set amount of follow-ups each week.

- Finishing a book or podcast that feeds your mindset and gives you new strategies.

Each small victory sends a signal to your brain: "I am capable. I can do this." Our thoughts are incredibly powerful.

#2 - Surround Yourself with Mentors who Believe in You

While we are cultivating belief from within— it can first come from the people around you. This is why mentorship is crucial. A mentor provides you with the guidance, support, and perspective you might not have yet. They can help you see your potential even when you can't see it yourself. We say "borrow our belief, while you are growing it for yourself."

- **Look for someone who has already achieved what you aspire to.** They don't have to be a direct connection—mentorship can come from books, courses, or podcasts.

- **Set up regular check-ins with a mentor or accountability partner.** Even a quick weekly call to discuss progress or offer a new perspective can keep you grounded and motivated.

#3: Commit to Non-Negotiable Daily Actions

We often say your daily routine takes you straight to your dreams. What are the most important activities that if nothing else got done would move your business forward? Establish non-negotiable daily actions, like adding names to your contact list, approaching new prospects, setting appointments, and following up. Use an accountability sheet of some form to track your activities. This can also give you clear data to know what skill sets you can improve on.

Coach's Notes: Leah's emphasis on non-negotiable daily actions is a masterclass in creating success. The beauty of these actions lies in their simplicity—they're not overwhelming but entirely doable. What's one non-negotiable action you can commit to today that will move your business forward?

Consistency builds momentum, and momentum reinforces belief. The size of the action matters less than the habit of showing up.

Making Your Belief Unshakeable

With a strong foundation of belief in place, the next step is to make it unshakeable. Belief is essential, but it needs to be fortified to withstand challenges, setbacks, and the negativity that can arise along your journey. In network marketing, belief is your anchor—it fuels your actions and keeps you motivated through both the highs and the lows.

But how do you make this belief truly unbreakable, especially when faced with the inevitable missed goals, periodic self-doubt and external negativity? We are in the people business even with strong belief, everything doesn't always go as planned.

Just as you've built your belief, you can strengthen it by nurturing confidence. These practices will help protect and expand your belief, empowering you to face obstacles with resilience and conviction.

#1: Eliminate Confidence-Killers

The first step is identifying and cutting out the influences that erode your confidence. This could be negative people, unproductive habits, or even consuming too much bad news. You might not realize it, but these sources of negativity quietly drain your energy, leaving you less motivated to tackle your goals. Here's what you can do:

- **Reduce exposure to negativity.** If watching the news or scrolling through social media leaves you feeling drained, limit your time doing those activities.

- **Distance yourself from negative people.** If certain individuals constantly bring you down, reduce your interactions with them. Surround yourself with those who lift you up and believe in your vision.

- **Replace bad habits with confidence-building ones.** For instance, replace the time spent on negative activities with reading personal development books or listening to podcasts that inspire you.

#2: Feed Your Confidence with Personal Development

Never stop learning and growing. One of the most effective ways to build confidence is through daily personal development. By consistently feeding your mind with positive, empowering content, you begin to shift your mindset from one of fear and doubt to one of belief and possibility.

Practical Action: Create a Personal Development Routine

- **Commit to at least 30 minutes of personal development every day.** This could be reading a chapter of a book, listening to a podcast, or watching motivational videos.

- **Choose content that aligns with your goals.** For example, if you struggle with rejection, focus on learning how to handle objections or build emotional resilience.

- **Keep a journal to reflect on key takeaways from your personal development journey.** This practice reinforces the learning and strengthens your confidence.

#3: Protect Your Environment

The environment you create—physically, mentally, and socially—has a direct impact on your confidence. If you're constantly surrounded by people or things that undermine your belief in yourself, it will be much harder to stay confident. Here's how to design an environment that fosters confidence:

- **Create a workspace that inspires you.** Set up a designated area for your work that is clutter-free, well-lit, and energizing. Surround yourself with things that motivate you, like vision boards, quotes, or pictures of people who inspire you.

- **Surround yourself with positive influences.** Spend time with people who encourage and challenge you to grow. Attend events, masterminds, or online groups where you can connect with like-minded individuals who are also striving for success.

- **Be intentional about your inputs.** Every day, you are taking in information that either supports your confidence or drains it. Be selective about what you allow into your mind. Focus on inputs that help you build confidence—whether that's through media, conversations, or content you consume.

Coach's Notes: Protecting your environment is more than just a productivity hack; it's about creating a space where belief can thrive. Leah's suggestion to be intentional with your inputs—what you listen to, watch, and read—is transformative for staying focused on your vision. How can you refine your environment to better support your goals today?

#4: Visualize Your Success

One of the most powerful confidence-building techniques is visualization. When you vividly imagine your future success, you train your brain to believe it's possible, even before you achieve it. This daily practice can significantly boost your confidence, especially when facing challenges.

Practical Action: Create a Daily Visualization Habit

- **Spend a few minutes each day visualizing your ideal future.** What does success look like for you a year from now? Where are you living? Who have you impacted? How does it feel to have achieved your goals?

- **Be specific and emotional in your visualization—engage all of your senses.** The more real it feels, the more confident you will become in your ability to achieve it.

- **Pair visualization with affirmations.** Repeating positive statements about yourself, such as "I am capable of achieving my goals" or "I am confident in my abilities," reinforces your belief in yourself.

Building unshakeable belief is a journey, and while each of these tips can strengthen your foundation, sometimes real growth happens when you put them to the test in your own life. To see these ideas in action, let's look at Sarah's story. Sarah was a mom and a new business partner, struggling with inconsistent results and growing doubts about her path. Through guidance and practical adjustments, she found a way to focus on what she could control, engaged her family in her journey, and made her belief in herself and her work a much stronger foundation. Here's how Sarah applied these principles to turn her business around.

Practical Application with Sarah

I started work with a wonderful woman named Sarah. She started in her new business but wasn't seeing the results she hoped for. Her belief dwindled, her routine became inconsistent, and she often skipped approaches or follow-ups. Each missed goal seemed to prove she wasn't cut out for success, leading to a spiral of self-doubt. As a mom of 3, she also felt guilt for the time she spent working on her business and not with her kids.

We met and came up with a plan to help her get out of her rut and get her belief back to where it was when she started. Sarah decided to shift focus from outcomes to process. She committed to 90 days of focusing solely on activities she could control, like building relationships, making approaches, follow-ups, and personal development. They also talked about how she could bring her family into her work on her business. The following is a summary of the plan they came up with to change the trajectory of her business.

#1: Create a Schedule and Make it Sacred
Treat your business like a job—except you're the boss. Designate non-negotiable work hours and track tasks on a calendar. Let your family know these hours are for focused work.

#2: Focus on Income-Producing Activities (IPAs)
Prioritize tasks that impact income, like contacting prospects, and avoid busywork. Work in 15-minute increments, concentrating on IPAs.

#3: Create Accountability
Accountability helps maintain progress, especially when motivation dips. Find an accountability partner with similar goals and a similar business stage. Set up regular check-ins and decide on rewards for consistent effort over a month.

#4: Include Your Family in Your Business
Plan a meeting with your spouse and kids where you can share with them what you are working on and why it's meaningful for your family. Share with them how you will be helping others along the way. Plan a special night out or fun thing you can do together when you work your plan and hit some of your goals. Help them to be a part of it and see you persevere, even when things don't go perfect. This is an incredible gift you can give you children, helping them learn lessons in goal setting, hard work, and personal growth.

Believe, Act, and Build Unshakeable Success

Sarah's story illustrates how a foundation of belief, combined with consistent action and confidence, can drive powerful results in network marketing and beyond. By actively strengthening your belief, protecting your confidence, and committing to a routine that prioritizes meaningful actions, you create a path toward lasting success.

Growth unfolds at the edge of your comfort zone, where you confront doubts, face challenges head-on, and hold firm to your vision. Remember, success is a choice—built through daily actions, persistence, and the unshakeable belief that you're capable of reaching your goals.

"It's not about the money. It's about who you become in the process, and who you help along the way, the money is a bi-product of those two things."

— Travis Flaherty

TRAVIS FLAHERTY

- Personally enrolled over 1,000 people in my career.

- Generated hundreds of millions of dollars in organizational sales.

- Seven Figure annual earner.

- Network Marketing Hall Of Fame Inductee (2023).

- Married 24 years with six beautiful children, 3 grandchildren.

Seven Figure Secrets: A Masterclass in Digital Entrepreneurship

What if I told you that the secrets to building a seven-figure business don't require overly complicated strategies or expert-level skills? You might think you could never be, do, or communicate like someone you admire on social media. Here's the good news: you don't have to!

Digital entrepreneurship is about being authentically, beautifully, and uniquely you. You've had experiences no one else has lived, overcome challenges that seemed insurmountable, and endured pain that taught you wisdom. This equips you to help others facing similar struggles.

Coach's Notes: Travis's wisdom reminds us that authenticity isn't just a trait—it's your superpower in digital entrepreneurship. You don't need to mimic others to succeed. Lean into your story, your strengths, and your experiences. What makes you unique is what will resonate most with your audience.

Not only *can* you be an online influencer; I'm sharing a digital blueprint that's allowed my wife and me to be fully present with our children, travel the world, and live a life by design.

It's all about mindset, consistency, and cultivating real relationships with your audience. In this chapter, I'll break down the exact steps I used to go from being broke after the 2009 crash to becoming a top earner in digital entrepreneurship and network marketing. These principles have helped me sponsor over 1,000 people, generate millions in sales, and build a business in over sixty countries.

The Rise of the Micro-Influencer

The digital marketing landscape has shifted. Today, micro-influencers—those with smaller, more engaged followings—are shaping buying decisions in ways big brands can't. Businesses are seeking authentic connections, and micro-influencers deliver.

With 1,000 to 100,000 followers, micro-influencers dominate the marketing scene. Their secret? Authenticity and trust. Studies show millennials trust product recommendations from influencers more than from celebrities, and micro-influencers generate up to 60% more engagement than larger influencers because their followers see them as relatable and genuine.

I didn't start with a huge audience. But I built relationships. I showed up authentically, and people trusted my recommendations. I wasn't just selling—I was offering real value. This approach helped me grow my audience and build a brand that people believe in.

This didn't happen overnight. I once attended a seminar where a well-known speaker captivated the audience. He had his own style: brash, fast-talking, and bold. I thought, "I need to be more like him." I started mimicking his style online, but it wasn't me. Not only did it feel unnatural, but I lost connection with my audience. Authenticity is key; pretending to be someone else will push people away faster than anything.

Side note: There's nothing wrong with learning from mentors and picking up positive habits, but always stay true to yourself.

What I learned is that you don't need millions of followers to build a successful digital business. You need trust, which is built by consistently delivering value and being genuine.

Too many digital entrepreneurs think they need to go viral or have tens of thousands of followers to succeed. They pretend to be something they're not. Or worse, they're afraid to be who they are. They focus on the wrong metrics and miss the opportunity to build real connections.

Stop chasing numbers. Stop trying to appeal to everyone, and please, stop buying likes, followers, and fans. This only hurts your engagement in the long run. Focus on building relationships. Go deep, not wide. It's the quality, not quantity, that counts. Engage with your audience, listen, and provide real value. The more authentic you are, the more they'll trust you. With trust comes credibility, and with credibility, you have solvency.

The Truth is Good Enough

Credibility in marketing comes down to one thing: being truthful. The truth is powerful, and it's good enough. Too often, people exaggerate, overhype, or make false income claims, believing it will attract more attention. But this only tarnishes their brand. When credibility is lost, it's very difficult to regain. People sense authenticity—and they can also sense when something doesn't feel right. Be transparent and honest in your marketing. The truth will resonate with the right audience and build a stronger, lasting brand.

Compound With Consistency

If there's one thing I've learned, it's this: consistency is your secret weapon. The daily habits you build are the foundation of your business. Success isn't built in a day—it's built every single day.

The key is your Daily Method of Operation (DMO). Here's what my typical day looks like:

- **1 hour of content creation:** Provide value through educational, inspirational, or entertaining content.

- **1 hour of starting conversations:** Build relationships in the DMs and engage authentically.

- **2-3 hours of calls/zooms:** Present, follow up, and close deals.

- **1 hour of personal growth:** Read, listen, or learn something new.

- **1 hour of exercise:** Keep your body in shape. When you feel good, you do good.

Coach's Notes: Consistency is the secret ingredient most people underestimate. Travis's DMO is a practical framework that transforms small, daily actions into monumental results over time. What does your DMO look like? Start small, track it, and watch the momentum grow.

By sticking to a routine, I transformed my business. It's not about talent—it's about showing up daily. Small actions lead to big results when done consistently. Many people give up too soon, expecting instant results, but success comes from commitment.

I challenge you to stick to a daily routine focused on content creation, relationship building, and personal growth. Do this for 365 days, and you'll see a transformation most people only dream of.

From Transactional to Transformative: The Mindset Shift

In digital entrepreneurship, there's a big difference between those who make a little money and those who build empires. It comes down to mindset. Top earners don't focus on quick wins; they focus on creating transformative value for their audience.

Coach's Notes: After knowing Travis for over fourteen years, one truth stands out: his ability to shift from transactional to transformational thinking is incredible. What value can you provide today that genuinely helps others? Remember, dollars follow value—not the other way around.

Many approach social media with a transactional mindset, wanting a quick sale or a new recruit. But this is short-sighted. Real leaders understand that *dollars follow value.* The formula is simple: T + A = C (Time + Authenticity = Credibility). The longer you show up and provide value, the more people will trust you.

In the early days, I was focused on getting quick sales. But when I shifted my mindset to focus on genuinely helping my audience, my business transformed. People trusted me because I wasn't just selling—I was invested in helping them succeed.

Developing a Content Marketing Strategy

Traditional marketing is less effective today. Your followers want more. That's where content marketing comes in. Smart marketers know content is king, but *value* is queen.

Content marketing is about building relationships, providing value, and educating your audience. It's not about pushing products. It's about making your audience smarter and better equipped to solve their problems.

Research shows 85% of entrepreneurs use content marketing, but fewer than half think they're good at it. Why? Because it requires vulnerability. You have to give without expecting immediate returns. Teach, entertain, and inspire—without the hard sell. I didn't get here by constantly pushing products. I built a community by consistently creating content that helped my audience. I shared my story, my challenges, and my lessons. By doing so, I earned their trust.

Your content should focus on solving problems, educating, or inspiring your audience. The more value you provide, the more loyal they'll be. Many on social media treat content as an afterthought, posting sporadically without a strategy. Develop a content strategy focused on teaching, entertaining, informing, or inspiring. Serve your audience, and your business will thrive.

Every audience is different. Over the years, I've learned that real connections come from focusing on what resonates emotionally. People crave authenticity; they want to be spoken to, not sold. When you share your heart, struggles, victories, and growth, people listen. They connect with the human side of your story.

Servant Leadership Over Salesmanship

People need more than just another product or income claim. With inflation, rising costs, and families feeling the pinch, the idea of multiple income streams is a necessity. But more than that, people seek peace of mind. As digital marketers, we tap into this by being real—showing how the opportunities we've found impact our lives, not just financially but in terms of peace of mind and freedom. That's marketing that connects on a deeper level.

Nobody wants to be *pitch slapped*. They don't want to be sold to; they want to know how what you're offering can make their lives better. Focus on the real impact your journey has had, be honest about challenges and victories, and lead with service.

If you're in digital marketing, remember: people connect with stories, truth, and leadership that puts their well-being first. They don't want to be sold to; they want to know how what you're offering can make their lives better. Focus on the real impact your journey has had, be honest about challenges and victories, and lead with service.

In a world driven by hype, *authenticity is your greatest asset.*

These are the secrets: Mindset, truthfulness, consistency, strategic content, adding value, serving over selling and building authentic relationships. Master these principles, and you'll succeed in the world of digital entrepreneurship. The tools are in your hands. *The question is, are you ready to use them?*

"Taking complete ownership of your outcomes by holding no one but yourself responsible for them is the most powerful thing you can do to drive your success."

— Gary W. Keller

JENNIFER VOSS

- Top 1% Earner.

- Earned 5 All-Expense paid trips in 6 years.

- Three-time conference stage recognition.

You Are the Power: Coachability and Radical Ownership

If I were to ask you to name the greatest basketball player of all time, there might be a handful of names with which you'd respond. One of those names, whether or not you're a sports fan, would probably be Michael Jordan.

Michael Jordan, arguably one of the greatest of all time, both at the game and in branded marketing, has said of himself: "My best skill was that I was coachable." Yet no one can deny his success was entirely his own.

What if unlocking your success isn't dependent on some innate talent you have (or don't have), but rather on becoming more coachable—while taking full responsibility for your results?

Everyone knows that Michael Jordan had incredible physical skill. So much in fact, that it's fair to say he was a better basketball player than most, if not all, of his coaches. Why would this innately talented individual not only accept coaching, but count it as so causal to his success?

Let's take this opportunity to define **coachability**.

Coachability is the combination of mindsets and behaviors for continuously integrating feedback and new information to drive growth and change within ourselves.

With our example of Michael Jordan, I'm sure there are several reasons he valued the skill of coachability above all others, but two most certainly are:

- He trusted that someone observing him could give him feedback that he couldn't see himself.

- He trusted that his coaches had experience with and a view of the big picture, and of what it takes to reach long-term success.

Let me take you back to a pivotal moment in my own journey in direct sales. A couple of years ago, I was feeling plateaued and stagnant after the roller-coaster success that came from the pandemic and its aftermath. My team was not seeing the (somewhat easy) success to which they'd become accustomed, and I was doubting my ability to guide them. When midnight on month-end was hours away, I sent a video message to my mentor, Anita, to let her know that we just weren't going to hit our goal.

I did not take her response well—initially.

"Jenn, I want you to go back and listen to that message again," she said. "Listen to yourself. Listen to what you've decided for you and your team."

My defenses kicked in. *"I know what I said; I don't have to listen again!"* But something prompted me to listen. As I replayed my words, I didn't like what I heard.

I heard someone who was sucking all the air out of the room. I heard someone who felt sorry for herself, and was coming from a place of a lot of excuses—most of them based on what other people were doing or not doing. NOT someone who had power over her own life. Not someone who recognized that she WAS the power.

When I sent my original message, I felt that I was just being pragmatic. Just stating facts. But the truth—that I couldn't see—was that I had decided on defeat and then sought evidence for that belief. Then my energy and actions followed that belief, and almost made it a reality.

Despite the "facts" that I initially thought predicted otherwise, our team did reach our goal that month. When the belief shifted, I was able to creatively think of ways I could reach out, motivate, remind, support—and all coming from a place of, and with an energy of, belief. But I needed that mirror held up to me—almost literally, with video text—to see how I had blinded myself.

If we hadn't reached our goal—because we've had months since then when we haven't—wouldn't I still have been a better leader, not speaking from assumed defeat? Yes, and a resounding yes.

Coach's Notes: Moments like Jennifer's remind us that leadership starts with self-awareness. When your energy aligns with belief, it creates momentum that inspires action. Reflect on how your mindset may be influencing your team and adjust as needed.

That moment of self-reflection was a turning point, and one that I could have easily missed if I didn't fight my urge to defend or excuse or ignore.

Coaching isn't just about mindset or belief. Sometimes it can look like suggestions of very practical action steps. At a different point in my career, I was feeling overwhelmed by my schedule and task lists. My mentor suggested that I track my time for the week so I could see where I was spending my hours. Once again, my initial response was not exactly to be coachable. Since I was already expressing that I didn't have enough time, why would I need another task?

I bet you can see where this is going. I decided to track my time, and it was eye-opening. Now it's an integral part of my success habits so I can make sure that where my time is going aligns with my values and priorities.

I was the one that needed to do the work, but if I held fast to defending my position of being "too busy" instead of taking her practical suggestion, I would have remained blind to where my time was actually going.

To be clear: Being coachable is not about surrendering your authority or relying solely on the guidance of others. In fact, quite the opposite. Instead, it's about recognizing that you alone have the ability to shape your path. You have the ability to seek out feedback and training— and implement it. You have the ability to decide how you respond to challenges. And none of it depends on our upline or even your home office / corporate support.

Coach's Notes: Coachability paired with ownership is the ultimate formula for growth. Take a moment to reflect: Are you fully leveraging the feedback you've received, or are you holding back? Progress begins with taking personal responsibility for your success.

This realization should be liberating! You have unlimited tools and resources at your disposal; all you need to do is be willing to learn and grow.

Many people enter network marketing not just with grand ambitions, but also with the personality and social network that would seem to predict success; and yet they hit walls when faced with setbacks. That problem often lies in a fixed mindset—retreating into excuses rather than embracing the learning opportunities that come with feedback, or refusing to own the responsibility to seek that feedback.

Within your specific company, it's certainly valuable to take advantage of upline/enrolling structure. But what if you don't have supportive leaders? What if you've lost levels above you and now feel like you're flying solo? Are you off the hook for seeking coaching?

Absolutely not!

A great place to look is for other people anywhere within your company who are topping the leaderboards for sales and enrolling, and consistently maxing out the compensation plan.

Observe these things:
- What do they consistently do?
- Where do they put their time?
- Where DON'T they put their time?
- What is their mindset and attitude? (This can be evident from their personal postings as well as their business posts.)
- How do they let perceived negatives affect them?

Then ask yourself the most important question: *Am I willing to work to do the same?*

If you are, find someone you can ask for feedback, and give them true permission to give it. Actively ask for constructive criticism from your upline and peers. Reach further up your team tree, or reach out to sideline sisters, or find a pacing partner with another company.

Beyond our own companies, there are myriad books, networking groups, and online trainings (free and paid) from which you can receive instruction, feedback, and accountability. YOU have the power to find and implement the things of value you find there.

As you begin this process of seeking additional perspectives, here are some foundational skills to being truly coachable.

- **Listening**
  This is truly an acquired skill with mindset work behind it. Learning to hear without defensiveness or "they don't understand" feelings leaves us open to hearing helpful critique, good advice, or direction for self-reflection.
  Seeking to understand, rather than seeking to respond, is a foundation of coachability.

- **Correct Assumptions**
  We need to check the assumptions that we're starting with. If you're receiving coaching from your upline or corporate trainers, I can guarantee that they want you to do well. That's just how our industry works!
  But even if we're talking about some other coach or trainer, or a successful person you'd like to emulate and learn from, they are sharing their skills, their time, and their insight for a reason. It's not to be judgy, or critical, or to make anyone feel less-than. It's to help YOU succeed.
  Coming from the assumption that coaching and feedback is for your own good makes hard pills easier to swallow.

- **Not Making Excuses**
  We love to think, "They're not excuses, they're reasons." But here's the thing: If they don't propel you forward—if they're not driving to a solution—they probably don't need to be said.

Coach's Notes: Excuses often feel justified, but they don't create solutions. When faced with challenges, ask yourself, "What is one small action I can take to shift this?" Small steps forward break the cycle of stagnation and lead to progress.

They serve only to cement you further in whatever situation you're making the excuse about anyway! (And this includes "if only," "I just wish," etc.)

Research shows that 95% of our thoughts are repetitive, and 80% are negative! Believe me, you don't need to repeat that excuse again. It does not serve you.

But we can do the hard work to actually change our neural pathways. While that is a huge topic, a great place to start when we go down the excuse road is to HALT, and ask ourselves, "Is this useful?"

Notice it's not, "Is this true?" or "Do I really feel this way?" Just, "Is this useful?" If not, challenge yourself to find a new response.

This will not feel natural at first! In my time as a fitness trainer, I would ask my clients to do many things that didn't feel natural. But over time, both the muscles and the brain learned these new—and better—patterns.

If you challenge yourself and your brain to have to come up with a different response, it will. But it is real work.

The intersection of coachability and ownership is the fundamental view that there is always a new perspective or something you can learn, and you are capable of learning it and responsible for implementing it.

If you're ready to take on that responsibility, start NOW.

I mean, right now.

The 70-20-10 Rule in Leadership Development tells us that 70% of our learning happens from "challenge assignments." That means implementing and getting experience. Seventy percent of what you're going to learn and how you're going to grow is going to come from your own DOING, messy or not. It's important that when you see or learn an activity/behavior/habit of success, you don't just underline it in a book or jot it down in your notebook, but implement it. Then of course get some accountability and be coachable with the feedback.

So, as we close, here are some questions to ask yourself:

- What is a skill, habit, or mindset I need to develop to elevate my business?

- Where or from whom can I learn more and ask for guidance?

- Reach out to that person, or join that online community, or find that in-person networking group, or secure that training (and schedule time in your calendar to DO the training) today.

While being coachable by definition speaks to the fact that there is a coach—or at least a trainer or teacher—it must always be YOU that is committed to your growth and owning your results. You cannot outsource it to others. Because YOU are the power.

"Rock bottom was my trampoline."

– Bethany Dawn Jury

BETHANY DAWN JURY

- 4,000 customers in 2 years.

- 3 company global trips.

- 3 leadership trips.

- 11 years sobriety.

- Circle of excellence leader.

- Global top enroller.

Divine Intersections: God's Hand in Our Digital Connections

We live in a different era for making money in network marketing; an era that offers more opportunities. Personal parties are a thing of the past. There is a major disconnect between human interaction, the cause of which has been dependent on devices to communicate with each other. Just look at McDonald's... more often you are seeing a screen over a person. In instances where we run into problems, there's no one to talk to about the solution—you're stuck on hold while glitches are worked out. But here's a thought: what if God is still working behind these digital scenes, guiding us just as He does in the rest of our lives?

In the vast expanse of the digital universe on platforms like Instagram, Facebook, and TikTok, every like, comment, and follow can seem like minor blips on the screen. But what if there's a divine orchestrator behind these connections?

A few years ago, during a tough time in my sobriety journey, I made a simple online comment on a post about recovery from addiction. I wasn't expecting much, but someone responded. This wasn't just any response—it felt like a message sent directly from God. As if He had directed this person my way to share what I needed to hear. We started chatting, and this person not only became a friend but also introduced me to the world of network marketing with products that aligned perfectly with my journey. This was no accident; it was a divine setup. Thanks to this connection, I found a path that helped strengthen my sobriety and led me to help others in their battles too.

When I embraced the notion that God intercedes in our digital interactions, each connection became more than a simple network expansion—it transformed into a potential relationship within my business and personal life. This shift in perspective can enrich your online engagement making every interaction a meaningful exploration of what God might be unfolding for you. It's incredibly impactful to think about how we can serve the people we connect with, identifying what gifts we have that might benefit them and considering what they might offer us. After all, I wouldn't be at the company I am now, if I had been closed off to new opportunities and stuck with my old company. God sent that opportunity.

Digital connections through conversations can lead to powerful exchanges that support not just a business relationship but also a spiritual comradeship. The more this starts happening, the clearer it becomes that it's not a coincidence; it's a clear instance of God's guidance, connecting you with someone who needs to hear your story just as much as you needed to share it. Additionally, you'll find that the products you share with them will likely help their journey too, showing how what we offer can align with our stories, which is important because it's rare that we stay somewhere just for the compensation plan alone.

Imagine every like, comment, or follow as a potential hint from God. He's not distant; He's actively involved in our online worlds, guiding us towards people and opportunities. Sometimes, these connections offer support; other times, they open doors we never expected. By believing that God has a hand in our digital interactions, every online meeting can turn into a meaningful relationship.

Coach's Notes: If you believe in God this chapter is perfect for you! Divine guidance often works through small, ordinary actions. Take time to reflect on your last meaningful digital connection—was it really just a coincidence? Let this perspective reshape the way you approach every message and comment.

The core message is clear: God is actively involved in our digital interactions. He uses our online platforms as tools to bring us together with others for mutual support, growth, and fulfillment of His purposes. Your mess is your message. Your transformation is someone else's hope. Yet, many of us overlook this divine hand in our digital dealings, often viewing online connections as solely pragmatic or serendipitous, missing the spiritual significance that these interactions may hold.

HOW DO YOU DO THIS?

1. **Seek Divine Intentions:** Start each online session with a prayer or intention. Ask God to guide your interactions. Approach every digital interaction with the mindset that God has a purpose for it. This means being open to finding deeper meanings and connections in what might otherwise seem like casual online engagements.

2. **Share Authentically:** Be real. Share your struggles and victories, especially about overcoming addiction. Your story could be the hope someone needs today. Reflect your faith, spirituality, however this chapter translates to you, and your journey openly in your digital communications. By sharing your true self, including your challenges and victories—like those in sobriety—you invite others into a more meaningful dialogue that can reveal God's purposes in your connection.

Coach's Notes: Approaching your digital efforts with faith changes everything. By starting each session with prayer or intention, you align your work with something greater than yourself, which infuses every interaction with purpose.

3. **Cultivate Patience and Listening:** Go beyond the surface. When chatting online, listen for God's voice. Maybe there's a reason you've crossed paths with someone. Use the Voice Message feature. Foster conversations that go beyond surface level. Listen for hints of God's workings in the lives of others. Hints of their experience crossroading with your experience, and dot that "i" to make the connection. By engaging deeply, you allow the space for divine intersections to be revealed and understood.

4. **Acceptance and Letting Go of Control**: We don't need to control every online interaction. Sometimes, the best approach is to let go and trust that God has a plan for every connection we make. Recognize that it's not our job to know why we were connected with someone online; our role is to trust that there's a reason for it. Embrace each connection with an open heart, letting go of the need to control the outcome. This is most important. It takes the pressure away from making a sale, and puts us in a place of service.

5. **Engage Proactively**: Visit their profiles, comment on their stories, and view their posts. This active engagement helps to uncover why you were connected. Then, reach out with a personalized message that ties back to your story and what you do, which can often reveal how your offerings could be of help.

Coach's Notes: This chapter is very deep. I want to add on to some of the incredible things Bethany has said. Connection doesn't stop at a single message. Dive deeper by engaging meaningfully with someone's content—this active effort can often uncover the reason behind the divine intersection of your paths.

6. **Facilitate Organic Interest**: Actively engage with others' content. Your genuine interest can turn a simple interaction into a deeper relationship and even open doors to share about your products naturally. By investing time in getting to know them and showing genuine interest in their content, you encourage a natural curiosity about what you offer. It gets you in their algorithm. Rather than pushing for a sale, share information in a way that makes them ask about your products or services, effectively placing you in their digital algorithm to keep you visible.

In closing, navigate the digital world with the confidence that God is orchestrating your connections behind the scenes. Trust in His timing and purpose, and approach each new online encounter as a potential divine play that He has a hand in dealing. I never would have thought that turning my mess into my message would be my way of income when I was scraping pennies under a couch to buy my next half-gallon before noon. But here I am. And here you are, too.

God is truly in every detail of our lives—even in the digital realm. Embrace this journey with faith, and witness how your digital interactions transform into channels of divine connection, where you see it was all a part of His plan!

Embrace this journey with faith, and witness how your digital interactions transform into channels of His works, where you see it was His plan all along!

"*No journey is too difficult if we dare to believe in your own strength and surround yourself with the right people.*"

— Ursula Hallin

URSULA HALLIN

- Traveled to 10 different countries in one year with my best friend.

- Spoke on the same stage as Rob.

- Learned English in less than a year, went from an uneducated burnt out girl to a successful, strong woman.

- Reached the top position in my company in the first week and the next time in the third week in the company.

- First influencer into Europe for our company, with now a team of over 5,000 people.

From Darkness to Connection: My Journey to Self-Acceptance and Success

It is often said that life's journey isn't always straightforward or easy. For me, it began in a darker place than I could ever understand as a child. I grew up as an introverted girl, often misunderstood, and my early years were marked by a deep sense of not belonging. Dyslexia, and possibly undiagnosed ADD, made every day a struggle. Schoolwork was a challenge, and the bullying I faced only reinforced my feeling of inadequacy.

The teachers didn't believe in me, and some even said I would never amount to anything. Perhaps it was their words that ignited a burning desire within me to prove them wrong. But it took a long time before I realized that there was nothing wrong with me — that having dyslexia and ADD wasn't an obstacle to success. I wasn't broken, just misunderstood. No adult saw that when I was a child, which led me to live with a lot of anxiety during my first twenty years. I was a child full of energy, but instead of being lifted up for my positive traits, I was pushed down.

Now, as an adult, I have a young daughter. In her, I see myself as a child. She is just like I was—full of life and energy, and incredibly kind. There is nothing wrong with her, just as there was nothing wrong with me. What was needed was understanding. As a mother, I am determined that she, and all other children like us, will be seen for the wonderful individuals they are. I want them to grow up in a world where their energy and creativity are celebrated.

From Darkness to Clarity – Finding My Path

During my early years, it felt like I was swimming against the current in life, getting nowhere. But deep inside, I always knew there was something more. A feeling that something bigger was waiting for me if I could only find the right path. I struggled for many years before discovering network marketing at the age of thirty four, then everything changed.

Coach's Notes: I have traveled the word with Ursula. She has been to my masterminds in Africa and Mallorca. Ursula's story shows us that life's greatest

transformations often start with a single brave step. Whether you're just beginning your journey or feel stuck, remember: the path to success is always within your reach, no matter where you start.

Going from being an invisible, quiet person to building a strong network of people was something I never expected. But in this world, I found something I had never experienced before—the freedom to be myself. Network marketing isn't just about selling products; it's about building relationships and helping others achieve their goals. It was as if a door opened, and I could suddenly see my potential in a way I had never before.

Today, I lead a team of over 5,000 people. Each individual in that network is a reminder of how far I've come. My passion lies not just in building successful businesses but in helping others find their own paths to success. By helping others grow, I have grown myself and found a new level of self-acceptance. It's a journey I could never have imagined as a child, but it now defines my life.

The Importance of a Mentor – Finding the Right Guidance

One of the biggest insights on my journey came when I truly understood the importance of having a good mentor. It's easy to feel lost when facing new challenges, and I often experienced that feeling in the early years of network marketing. But thanks to Angel Rodriguez and Lance Conrad, I learned how crucial it is to have the right coaching. They taught me that if you want to be great at something, you must work on both yourself and your personal development. If you want to become a professional at something, you need a coach who is a professional. Without a really great coach, you'll never reach your full potential.

Their advice was a turning point for me. Having a mentor who believed in me when I doubted myself gave me a strength I didn't know I had.

Their mentorship helped me grow, not just as an entrepreneur but also as a person. It made me understand my own value on a deeper level. When I saw how much I grew with their support, it became important for me to offer that same support to others.

Seeing others develop, reach their goals, and find their own way has become one of the greatest joys in my work. I have seen what's possible when you have the right support, and I want to be that mentor for others that Angel and Lance were for me. I believe we all have the potential to succeed, but we need the right guidance to get there.

Travel and Relationships – Finding a Soulmate

Network marketing has opened a world of opportunities for me, both professionally and personally. One of the most meaningful relationships I've built on this journey is with my friend Robin. From the moment we met, it felt like we had known each other forever. Our relationship quickly became something deep and meaningful—almost like we were soulmates.

The strong bond between us brought a sense of freedom and adventure. Within the first year of knowing each other, we traveled together to ten different countries. Each trip wasn't just an opportunity to explore new places and cultures but also a chance to deepen our friendship and have profound conversations about life. Those moments, traveling and sharing experiences, gave me a sense of having found a rare friendship that truly enriches my life.

The freedom to travel is something I've always dreamed of. But it's not just the freedom to see the world; it's the freedom to create a life where I get to do more of what I love. Through network marketing, I've created that freedom, and now I can also offer others the chance to do the same. It's not just about selling products; it's about giving people the tools to create their dream lives.

Coach's Notes: Imagine creating a life where freedom isn't just a dream but your reality. Ursula reminds us that the opportunities network marketing offers go beyond financial gain—they provide the freedom to live life on your terms and build meaningful connections along the way.

Health and Balance – The Key to Success

My journey has taught me that success isn't just about making money or building a large network. Success is equally about creating a lifestyle that supports both physical and mental health. For me, it's crucial to surround myself with people who bring positive energy and help me maintain balance in life.

Having the right people around you is key to feeling good and staying motivated. It's easy to get overwhelmed by life's demands, but with a strong support network, I always feel empowered. That balance is what I want to help others find as well—a balance between work, health, and freedom.

Swimming Against the Current – Having the Courage to Resist

Working in our industry can sometimes feel like swimming against the current. It's easy to just go with the flow, doing what feels easy, but to truly achieve success, you must be willing to go the extra mile. You have to be in constant motion, always taking initiative and doing the work. If you don't, you'll just be pulled back with the current.

Coach's Notes: Ursula's metaphor of swimming against the current is a great reminder that true growth requires effort and persistence. When you push through challenges instead of avoiding them, you build the resilience needed to reach new heights.

Being passive means standing still, but if you truly push yourself and dare to swim against the current, you can reach new heights. This insight has been crucial to my success. It has required me to step outside my comfort zone and continually strive to be better. That's the kind of effort it takes to succeed—not just in network marketing but in life.

The Journey Continues

My journey from a sense of darkness and uncertainty to finding my voice and success hasn't been easy. But every step has been worth it. I've learned that success doesn't come on its own. It takes hard work, courage, and a willingness to keep moving forward, even when it feels like everything is working against you.

Through network marketing, I've not only found a career I love, but I've also found myself. I've built relationships with people who lift me up and make me a better version of myself. If I can do it, so can you!

"Problems are a sign of progress and difficulties are a sign of destiny."

— Myron Golden

REBECCA WHITE

- Hitting Diamond and Double Diamond in record time.

- Over 4,800 team members in less than eighteen months.

Advancement Through Adversity: How to Teach Your Team to Overcome Disappointment and Truly Win

Unfortunately In life and business, adversity is inevitable. It's not something to be frightened of, it's actually a growth hack! After 43 years on this planet I have finally learned that How you respond to disappointment determines your success as a leader and that directly impacts the growth of your team. Leadership is the highest-paying skill and Network marketing is no exception—it's filled with the highest of highs and sometimes the lowest of lows.

But what if I told you that the key to true leadership and abundance in this profession lies in how you and your team navigate these challenges? I've built a six-figure business in less than twelve months not because everything went smoothly, but because I learned to thrive in adversity, turning obstacles into opportunities. Creating and developing my growth mindset wasn't an overnight process, but it has been one of the most rewarding journeys of my life.

Network marketing is more than just a vehicle for financial success; it's a journey of personal growth. The profession calls for true resilience, self-awareness, and the ability to rise above disappointment. It's an opportunity to heal, evolve, and step into the best version of yourself.

Before I achieved success in this industry, I was stuck in a victim mindset. Trauma from my past kept me reactive to every challenge, and I let disappointment define my worth. It wasn't until I began healing, releasing the energy of trauma, and stepping into my power that I saw real change—not only in my business but in my life. This business is amazing for those truly ready to leave behind the victim mentality and embrace the abundance, love, happiness, and wealth they *deserve*. It offers the education we don't get at school or in the office, it's a chance for next-level self-awareness, more responsiveness, and a higher level of consciousness. It is the ultimate transformation process, that you can also get paid for!

I started my journey like many others, I did have a little MLM PTSD due to a couple of failed attempts...but I really didn't understand the industry, or have the right mentorship which doesn't seem to help at all. When I saw this vision of my company, I was full of hope and excitement. But it wasn't long before the reality of disappointment hit. I had a six-month run of dreams and hit a six-figure plus income. Then the company ran out of stock for my country!!! It was a huge hurdle, the first of many. Teammates left, deals fell through, the prelaunch of my company wasn't smooth and they certainly didn't have everything perfect (does anyone?) and to be fair, I was constantly questioning myself. Growing up with a troubled early childhood and a lot of traumas made this even harder. Every setback felt like confirmation that I wasn't good enough. I was stuck in a reactive state, constantly trying to prove myself while feeling weighed down by fear and doubt.

But something shifted in me when I realized that I had the power to change my perspective. The words, "Emotions are great consultants and terrible CEO'S" constantly run through my head. I could either let adversity break me, or I could use it to build myself into the leader I was meant to be. Through healing, mindset work, and a deep commitment to growth, I transformed. I stopped seeing challenges as personal failures and started viewing them as opportunities for growth. "Here we Grow Again" is also a great phrase that is repeated on the daily, throughout this journey.

This shift didn't just change me—it transformed my business. I went from a trauma victim to a powerful entrepreneur who created a six-figure income, not by avoiding adversity, but by embracing it. I learned to respond to challenges rather than react, and this has been one of the most valuable lessons in leadership.

Coach's Notes: Imagine transforming adversity into the foundation of your success. Rebecca exemplifies how a mindset shift—from reactive to proactive—can revolutionize not just your business but your entire life. Challenges are no longer roadblocks; they become stepping stones to greatness.

Adversity is part of the journey, but it doesn't have to derail you or your team. Success in network marketing doesn't come from avoiding disappointment but from learning how to grow through it. The leaders who truly win are the ones who know how to guide their teams through the tough times and come out stronger on the other side.

In network marketing, disappointment is often seen as a roadblock. People get discouraged when their team members leave, when sales goals aren't met, When they don't re-rank, or when they're criticized by others in the industry. Many start internalizing these setbacks, feeling as though they are failures. This leads to reactivity: emotional responses, knee-jerk reactions, and a tendency to take things personally.

Coach's Notes: Rebecca's vulnerability in sharing her early struggles is a masterclass in turning pain into purpose. By acknowledging her challenges and leaning into tools like the Perspective Analysis Process, she shows us how leaders can guide their teams through adversity and emerge even stronger.

Without the right tools, this cycle can hold you back from growth. It can cause division within teams, foster miscommunication, and leave individuals feeling stuck. Then the ones that are not ready for real growth find themselves thinking the grass is greener... None of us wasn't to get a name for ourselves.

As a leader, you have to teach your team how to break free from the reactive mindset and adopt a more empowered, responsive approach.

One of the most effective strategies my mentor and coach, Steven Keller taught me to do and to help guide my team through disappointment is the **Perspective Analysis Process**. Self Awareness is the key to becoming the best version of yourself, it truly is about who you become along the way.

Coach's Notes: Rebecca's insights show us the transformative power of gratitude in the face of adversity. By shifting focus to what's going right, you cultivate resilience within yourself and your team,

creating a culture that thrives despite challenges. Pay attention to these three steps she will share that will help you out tremendously.

It's a simple, yet powerful, tool that can shift you and your team from reactivity to responsiveness. Here's how it works:

Step 1: Initiate a Solution-Oriented Dialogue

When a teammate is struggling or you're dealing with a tough situation, approach them by asking, "I have a solution if you're interested. Are you open to discussing it?" This invites them to engage in a constructive conversation rather than stay stuck in the problem.

Step 2: Use Pen and Paper for Clarity

Have them take out a piece of paper and draw a line down the middle. On one side, they write "What I know for sure" – this should include only the hard facts about the situation, without assumptions or emotions. On the other side, they write "What I can actually do about it." This process helps shift focus from the drama to the facts and allows for a clearer, solution-focused mindset.

Step 3: Identify Three Possible Outcomes

Typically, the situation will fall into one of three categories:

- The person doesn't want to solve the issue, in which case they're likely not ready to grow or unwilling to take responsibility. It's important here to ask for respect for your time.

- The situation wasn't as bad as it initially seemed, and this may indicate an area for growth or learning.

- They gain clarity, figure out how to fix it, and may even apologize for bothering you with the problem in the first place.

This process not only helps your team gain clarity on adversity but also shifts their thinking from reactive to proactive, encouraging them to focus on what they can control.

Let's be real, shit *happens*. Teammates leave, people criticize you, and sometimes others will even try to bring you down by poaching team members or cross-recruiting. This is the reality of network marketing, but it doesn't have to define your experience.

The key to coaching your team through adversity is helping them gain a new perspective. Encourage them to approach challenges with a sense of gratitude and power. Yes, challenges arise, but they are always opportunities for growth. Teach your team to see adversity as a chance to become stronger leaders, to improve communication, and to build resilience. It's not about avoiding the bad—it's about learning how to navigate through it with grace and strength.

One of the greatest lessons I've learned through my own journey is the power of gratitude. When faced with adversity, shifting focus from what's going wrong to what's going right can transform your entire experience. Gratitude is not just a mindset; it's a tool for elevating your consciousness and moving past negativity.

When you teach your team to approach adversity with gratitude and perspective, you create a culture of resilience. They stop taking things personally and start seeing every challenge as a stepping stone toward success. This is the key to truly winning in this business.

Adversity and disappointment are part of the journey in network marketing, and entrepreneurship but they are not the end. They are opportunities for growth, self-awareness, and leadership development. When you teach your team to shift their perspective, to move from reactivity to responsiveness, and to embrace the lessons within adversity, you create a culture of resilience and success.

The next time you or a team member faces a challenge, take out a piece of paper and do a perspective analysis. Focus on the facts, identify what can be done, and act from a place of clarity, not emotion. Lead by example, and watch your team rise to new levels of consciousness, growth, and power.

This industry is amazing for those who are ready to leave behind victimhood and step into the abundance, love, happiness, and wealth that they deserve. The opportunity is here, but it's up to you to make the decision to grow. You have the power to transform adversity into the foundation for your success. Are you ready to truly win?

"You can do, have, and become whatever you want in life."

— Tony Robbins

LORENA GABOR

- Team made millionaire.

- Number 1 team in 8 countries.

- Real estate investor and philanthropist.

How to Achieve Success Without Sacrificing Your Family, Health, and Values

How many times have you heard the phrase, "You need to sacrifice three years of your life to enjoy the rest of it?" It's a mantra that's spread everywhere—from social media to the so-called business gurus telling you to grind harder, sacrifice everything, and hustle your way to the top. But let me ask you this: Is that really how you want to live? Do you want to look back and realize you missed out on your family, your health, and the things that matter most—all in the name of "success"?

Coach's Notes: Too often, leaders get caught up in the narrative that hustle equals worth. Lorena's perspective reminds us that alignment and energy matter just as much—if not more—than effort. Share this insight with your team to help them redefine their approach to success.

What if I told you that success doesn't require giving up the things that make life meaningful? What if there was a way to build your dreams, achieve financial freedom, and create a life you love without sacrificing your happiness, health, or family? In this chapter, I want to share how I've done exactly that—by aligning my energy, living true to my values, and finding joy in the journey. You don't need to follow someone else's program, wake up at the crack of dawn, or work yourself to the bone.

When I was born, my parents were poor, but they had big dreams. They wanted to build a better future for me, and they worked tirelessly to make that happen. Their dreams came with a cost. They worked so hard that they couldn't be present during my childhood. Until I was twelve years old, I was raised by my grandparents. It was a beautiful experience in many ways—I was loved and cared for—but I missed my parents.

That's where my belief was born, I remember my father saying "we do it for you" and that's when I replied "It's not about how much money you make, but how you make it". If success comes at the cost of your time, your family, and your health, is it really worth it? I saw firsthand that even with good intentions, chasing success in a way that sacrifices what's most important can leave a void in your heart.

Through this experience, I realized that true success isn't about sacrificing everything to achieve it. Success should feel aligned, joyful, and fulfilling. It should support your values, not undermine them. But society often pushes the opposite idea: that to reach the top, you have to give up what matters most. I believed that for a while too, and it didn't serve me.

When I entered the workforce, both in traditional business and as an employee, I saw people around me burning out. They were sacrificing time with their families, neglecting their health, and running themselves into the ground for the sake of "success." It felt like no matter where I turned, there was no example of success without sacrifice. That's when I found network marketing.

Coach's Notes: Lorena's journey illustrates how crucial it is to challenge traditional notions of success. Consider asking yourself and your team: Are our goals aligned with the kind of life we want to live? Use this chapter as an opportunity to evaluate your approach to leadership and fulfillment.

At twenty five, I entered the industry looking for freedom, but even there, I encountered people pushing the same narrative—massive action at the expense of everything else. Deep down, I knew that wasn't the way I wanted to live.

It took me three years to align my approach and realize that success could be achieved differently. I began to focus on energy rather than just massive action. I discovered that when your energy is right, everything else falls into place.

This is my formula: *Success = Energy x Skills*

What does that mean? It means that instead of chasing after success with blind action, you focus on how you feel. You pay attention to your energy, and you make sure that what you're doing aligns with how you want to feel. You sharpen your skills, yes, but the energy behind your actions is what truly amplifies your results.

Energy – learn how to: Create it – Protect it – Share it

For me, this shift changed everything. I went from earning 1,000 euros a month to 10,000 in six months, then doubled that to 20,000 euros within the next six months. Today, I make five figures a week, and our team is number one in eight countries.

But the numbers aren't the most important part. What matters is how I got here—and how my team members got here. They're not burned out. They're not stressed to the point of breaking. They're enjoying what they do because we focus on energy first.

Don't get me wrong, we still had difficult moments, but in those moments we remembered what's important, to feel just a bit better and stay aligned with our values. Everything works out when you have this mindset and all the people, situations and circumstances that are not aligned with that energy will eventually get out of your life.

My Way - Unpopular Opinion

1. You don't need to wake up early or follow someone else's "success program." I wake up at noon, and we've built massive success. The only thing that matters is taking action toward your goals in a way that works for you.

2. The focus is ALWAYS on feeling good. When your energy is right, the actions are a natural consequence, and the results multiply.

3. I have preferences like wanting to reach a goal within a month, but I have zero attachment to those goals. If I don't hit them, it's okay because my goal is to connect as much as possible to the energy of "it's already done."

Practical Tips for Boosting Energy

1. **Check in with Yourself**: Several times a day, stop and ask, "How do I feel?" Your energy is your most valuable asset, so you need to stay connected to it. This practice will completely transform your life. It had the biggest impact on mine.

2. **Move Your Body**: Physical movement, whether it's walking, dancing, or even stretching, is an easy way to raise your energy instantly.

3. **Meditate or Pray**: Find stillness, connect with yourself, and quiet your mind. This will recharge your energy and help you stay focused.

4. **Step Outside**: Being in nature can uplift your energy in ways that are simple but profound.

5. **Practice Gratitude**: Focusing on what you're thankful for shifts your energy toward positivity, which then creates a ripple effect in your actions.

6. **Have Clarity**: Many times we feel overwhelmed because we lack clarity. Getting clear on your goals and your next steps will elevate your energy and make everything feel more manageable.

7. **Personal Development**: Never stop growing. Personal development keeps your skills sharp and your energy high, fueling long-term success.

Where Does Massive Action Fit In?

Massive action will happen naturally when your energy is aligned and your skills are sharp. You don't need to force it. Just imagine yourself, full of energy, connected to your goals and knowing exactly what you need to do. When you feel good and you know what you're doing, the action flows, you can't just wait, you'll "*just do it*" like Nike says. When your energy is high, the results will multiply.

Here's what I want you to take away: Ask yourself several times a day, "*How do I feel?*" This question is a powerful tool to keep you aligned with your energy and your well-being. When you feel the pressure building, step back and remember the bigger vision, how far you've come and what are your goals.

This is not just for you—this is something to share with your team. They will have moments of frustration and exhaustion, and it's your role as a leader to help them step back, take a break, and realign with the bigger picture. It's all about shifting energy, even in small steps. You can't go from feeling low to feeling great in one leap, but you can move from feeling low to feeling just a bit better. That's the key—small shifts that compound over time.

Switching Between Work and Family

One of the biggest challenges people face today is being fully present. When they're working, they're thinking about their family. When they're with their family, they're thinking about work. This constant mental juggling can drain energy and lead to feelings of sadness or frustration.

Coach's Notes: Lorena's advice about balancing energy across life's priorities is incredible. Encourage your team to reflect: Are they being intentional with their time? Remind them that alignment, not perfection, is the key to sustainable success and joy.

The key isn't about having a perfectly balanced life 100% of the time—that's impossible. But it is important to be able to mentally switch between work and personal life. This means putting intentional time, energy, and effort into all aspects of your life that matter: family, health, sport and wellness, business, and spirituality. All of them deserve your attention and energy in their own right.

Balanced Life and Energy

There are five key areas that deserve your time, energy, and effort: family, health, sport and wellness, business, and spirituality. No matter how busy life gets, it's crucial to put energy into all five areas. It's not about balance, but alignment. When you are aligned in these areas, success doesn't feel like a grind. It feels natural and fulfilling.

I've seen this happen firsthand with the people I work with. Many of the mothers in our team feel frustrated or burned out because they don't have enough time. It's our responsibility as leaders to check in with them, ask how they're feeling, and help them find solutions that ensure their well-being. The goal isn't just to create top leaders—it's to create leaders who still have strong, loving relationships with their families.

We don't want someone to be a top leader while their children stop speaking to them because they weren't present. It's possible to have both; success and a balanced life, but it requires the right mindset and approach.

Often, we think that as leaders, our job is to give solutions. But that's not true. Our job is to listen and help people discover their own solutions. Most of the time, they already know what they need to do—they just need to ask themselves the right questions.

This is where questions like "How do I feel?" and "How can I improve it?" become essential. Our role is to guide people in asking these questions and help them focus on the bigger picture, rather than getting caught up in their immediate emotions or frustrations.

The bigger picture is always more important than what's happening at the moment. As leaders, it's our duty to remind people of this and help them realign their energy to move forward with clarity and purpose.

In the end, it's not about how much we achieve, but how happy we are while we're achieving it. Success without joy is hollow.

I do believe that we can do, have and achieve everything we want in life! (on our terms)

"You've heard it said that T.E.A.M. means Together Everyone Achieves More. Don't forget the other acronym that comes into play in our industry: R.A.M.B.O. - Rarely Achieve Much By Oneself."

– Chuck & Tammi Gates

CHUCK & TAMMI GATES

- 8 Figure a year earners.

- Helped develop over 20 6 & 7 figure earners.

- Over 100,000 team members.

- Earned over $13 million in the network marketing industry.

- 35 year career network marketing.

ONE TEAM, ONE DREAM

What does an organization of over 100,000 associates and customers spanning thirty four countries and generating constant million dollar sales volume weeks have to do with being a team?

You've heard it said that T.E.A.M means Together Everyone Achieves More. Don't forget the other acronym that comes into play in our industry:

R. A. M.B.O Rarely Achieve Much By Oneself.

Let us start by introducing ourselves, We are Chuck & Tammi. We have three adult children who have all married well and have given us seven grandchildren. We are native Montanans and have been married to each other for forty five years. Over the last forty or so years, we have been to the top of three different network marketing companies while also kissing a lot of frogs!

Coach's Notes: Chuck and Tammi's story emphasizes that resilience and adaptability are key ingredients to long-term success. Have you noticed that every leader has had a set back and almost every leader is willing to share their struggles. This is a great lesson to learn!

The first company we went to the top of got their financing pulled out from underneath them, which led us to find our second company in 1994, building to the top yet again. Then they started making decisions that drastically affected our income and that of our team.

On a Sunday night fifteen years ago, two nights before Christmas at 9 pm, the sponsor of our third and current company followed the lead of her heart and called us. She had no clue what a devastating financial situation we had ended up in, but we will be forever grateful she acted on her prompting.

You may be thinking that we were able to build to the top of a third company because of the significant team we had built in our former companies, and all we had to do was bring them on over. Wrong! We were legally bound to NOT speak with our former team and unable to even disclose to them about what we were doing, so we started over with new people just like everyone does.

We've since developed Five Critical Elements to consider when choosing a network marketing company to partner with. One of the most important elements is field leader training & support systems. Eric Worre of Network Marketing Pro teaches that systems can buy people time while they build their skills. These systems can and should be built by field leaders for their teams.

Our Top 5 Team Building Support Systems:

1. **Daily Training Calls.** We have participated in leading this type call for the past fifteen years. Conducted each Monday to Friday morning, it is kept to a strict thirty minutes that starts and ends on time and our call is popular to listen to live. It's a morning call that just seems to kick everyone's day off right. We record it for those who can't make the live call and post it online so no-one ever has to miss one. Each call starts with a live product testimony interview followed by team announcements then a twenty minute training, The training follows an acronym we call A-LIFT. We routinely teach one letter of the A-LIFT process every day. Why do we teach this? Because it works! A stands for Attitude - it's the rock upon which you build your business! L is for list who are you going to talk to and share your remarkable product & business with? How are you going to do that? I is for Invite - you're going to invite them to learn more by using a tool, and you'll let the tool tell the story. F is for Follow Up. The Fortune is in the Follow Up! Lastly, T is for Teach your Team to do the same. It is not what YOU do but it's what you DUPLICATE! Each training represents one of these core skills in the list, and if you find yourself implementing this tip, we invite you to create your daily training system and develop a good acronym, too!!

2. **Communication Systems.** Communication among teams is key. No longer can we rely on only email to be our standalone form of communication with our folks. In this day and age your team will benefit by using as many communication outlets as you can: Private, Invitation-only Facebook Groups, team FB Pages, WhatsApp Groups, Facebook Messenger Groups; Text Messaging services, and automated "Welcome to the Team" campaigns are our favorites.

Coach's Notes: The emphasis on communication systems in this chapter is gold. Ask yourself and your team: Are we leveraging the best platforms to stay connected and aligned? Consistent communication can turn a group of individuals into a cohesive unit.

We teach our team to forward messages and announcements to their own teams.

3. **Recognition Systems.** You may have heard it said that many people do more for praises than they do for raises! Who doesn't like to see his or her own name up in lights? Our favorite team-building system for recognition is on Facebook. We add people to our recognition group when they enroll in our company and welcome them in a post with their picture. We make sure to tag them in the message with a post. All of their Facebook friends are able to see this message, so we like to create a curiosity post to draw their Facebook friends into the new enrollee's new business journey, Something like, "Mama's got a new biz in the house! Congrats [Tag name here] on starting this new journey! Looking forward to teaming up with you to help loads of other people!"

4. **Team Calls.** We encourage our up and coming leaders to gather their young, growing teams around the proverbial campfire regularly. These Zoom calls start out with a win for the week. Anyone is welcome to unmute and brag about what business building activity they are most proud of that week. They are also welcome to introduce any new members they've recently sponsored, This really encourages community among the team, and when they meet at events, they have a sense of each other's journeys and a family culture begins to develop. The win for the week is followed by WAM (weekly accountability meeting), announcements so everyone is on the same page and then maybe a message/story/business testimonies or tip from an upline or crossline leader.

5. **Team Events.** During our company-wide conventions and events, we host a team-wide event like a lunch or dinner so that, once again, folks can gather, talk, share ideas and tips, and network. We do special recognition outside of rank advancements and cover any special corporate announcements delivered during the company event so that everyone understands the promotions or incentives. We are also very clear about going over what the next event is and where we will all get together again. Our industry boils down to a simple skill of *moving people from event to event.* We have found that the host hotel or a nearby restaurant is an extremely economical venue to host these live events that coincide with your corporate events.

Whatever types of support and systems you develop, the top three rules are consistency, consistency, and consistency. In the absence of someone's confidence in their own skills, reliability will be your best friend. If you announce a weekly thirty minute call, make sure you do everything in your power to not cancel it; even if it means recruiting one of your leaders to run the call in your absence. Start on time and end on time. Having even the newest rookie on your team know what to expect from you and your support systems will increase their confidence in you, your company, and your products as well as confidence in their ability to share the products and business with others.

Don't try to reinvent the wheel. If your upline has some of these support systems for their teams, take advantage of them. We are always careful about how much time we are taking up during the week for those on our team. We try to remember that many of them are trying to fit building their business into the nooks and crannies of jobs, family, and other responsibilities and roles they have. The last thing we want to encourage a new leader to do is to duplicate something for their team that is already being successfully implemented by one or more or their upline leaders.

One last team tip is: Don't forget your spouse/significant other or family. "Team household" is one of the most important teams to build as you build your dream and business. You may have to prospect and recruit them like you would anyone else...ask them to do you a favor or honor you by looking at websites or watching company videos. Bring them on board with you. When our kids were younger we would bring them with us to meetings and events and we would include them by rewarding them for good behavior as we were beginning to see success. How about a big prize for them when we experienced a big rank advancement? A trampoline, maybe? Or a trip? We began to involve our children and grow their social skills by having them introduce us at small meetings or interact with restaurant wait staff by learning to pay the check. One time we came home after a meeting to recognize signs and balloons they had hung all over the house because we had advanced in rank that day! They really felt like the entire family had accomplished a goal. We believe we have raised amazing adult humans because of the people they were around and the skills they were a part of building while they were growing up.

Also, if you are working this with a spouse, take care to keep judgment, competition, or blame out of the game! Find your strengths and develop your weaknesses and release your partner to do the same. In our business, Chuck is great at meeting and finding people. He is genuine and sincere and people like him immediately and he can create rapport fast. But Chuck doesn't do technology much. He tells people that Tammi is a whiz at emails, Messenger, What's App, Facebook, or our back office. So we team up and cover each other's weaknesses. Tammi doesn't expect Chuck to learn tech, and Chuck doesn't whine that Tammi isn't prospecting enough. We like the mantra that a former mentor taught us years ago: he finds them, she winds them!

Coach's Notes: This final reflection reinforces an essential truth: true leaders uplift others to lead. Use this insight to foster a culture where every team member feels empowered to build and lead in their unique way.

Although we started this chapter talking about some pretty stellar accomplishments of our team, we want to be clear. We have so many leaders on our team that do team-building better than we do! If it weren't for the skills, efforts, and support systems that they have built for their teams, we couldn't even approach those stats and numbers from the first paragraph in this chapter! Those are simply a reflection of a group of amazing men and women chasing their dreams. We have linked arms together because R.A.M.B.O.-Rarely Achieve Much By Oneself.

When you can gather people around a common vision and support them in it, you can truly develop One Team. One Dream.

"Attitude is a little thing that makes a big difference."

— Unknown

RACHAEL LALJI

- 7 figure income earner.

- Number one in the company in 5 years.

- Co - host of the Mile High podcast.

- Company MVP 2024.

- Millionaire hall of famer.

The Power Within

This chapter isn't just about my journey; it's about our journey—the journey of discovering and harnessing the power that's already inside you. For me, network marketing was the vehicle that transformed my life, but the real fuel behind my success? That was something far deeper. It was the strength I didn't know I had, the resilience that carried me through sleepless nights, and the unwavering belief that I could create a better life for myself and my family. I didn't just find success in this industry; I found *power*—the power to believe in myself, the power to dream bigger than I ever thought possible, and the power to create a ripple effect that has touched countless lives.

The power of you isn't just about financial success or achieving accolades. It's about tapping into the unique strengths and gifts that only you possess.

Coach's Notes: Rachael's story reminds us of the importance of embracing our individuality. First know this for yourself and then make sure you share this with your team to encourage them to focus on their unique strengths, as those differences are often what set successful leaders apart.

Let me tell you a story about a friend of mine, Sarah. She always saw herself as average, just another face in the crowd. But one day, she realised her love for story telling and how it could captivate an audience. She started using this skill to connect with her network marketing team and guess what? Her team started to thrive. Sarah discovered her superpower and used it to inspire others.

Let me take you back a few years to when I first stepped into this industry. I was green, nervous, and full of doubt. I saw leaders on stage, talking about their success, and I couldn't help but think, "What do I have to offer? How can I compete with that?" But then, something clicked. I realized that those people weren't successful because they had something I didn't. They were successful because they embraced what made them unique. They didn't try to copy someone else's flair; they created their own. So, I started to dig deep, to find what made me, well, me. I uncovered talents I didn't even know I had, and I let those shine. Slowly, I saw how my team began to flourish—not because I was mimicking someone else, but because I was finally embracing my own power.

The point is simple: Recognise your uniqueness. Understand that you bring something to the table that nobody else can. Your individuality is not a hindrance, it's an advantage. Take a moment to list your unique qualities. What are your talents? Your passions? How can you use them to make a difference in your network marketing journey? Share your stories, insights, and experiences with your team. Your voice is powerful.

The Power To Be More

If you've made it this far into the book, it's clear you don't want to be average . You want more right? Let's get real for a second. If you've made it this far into the book, I'm guessing you're not looking to be average. You're here because you want more? Here's the thing, you have the power to be more. Right now, the most powerful ally you have is staring back at you every morning in the mirror.

You've been given an incredible vehicle—network marketing. You have the keys in your hand, but some of you haven't even turned on the ignition. Why? Because some of you still don't believe you're capable of driving this thing to its full potential. But here's the truth: nothing life-changing happens to average people. If you want something different, you have to become someone different. You have to believe you're more than what you've settled for so far.

Think about a time you hesitated to take a step forward. Maybe it was fear, doubt, or disbelief holding you back. For me, it was when I first started in network marketing maybe six or seven months in. I had the tools, but I was still too afraid to use them. That changed when I finally turned the ignition and took control of my journey. Remembering back to the first time I realized I was coasting. I was doing okay, hitting some goals, making some money, but deep down, I knew I was playing small. I was afraid to push harder, to take risks, to really put myself out there. Then, one day, I had a conversation with a mentor who asked me one simple question: "Are you living up to your potential?" It hit me like a ton of bricks because I knew the answer was no. From that day on, I made a promise to myself to stop settling. I started showing up differently—more focused, more driven, more willing to do the hard things. Guess what? My results exploded. You have the power to be more, but it starts with believing you can be. This isn't just about making more money or climbing higher in the ranks—this is about becoming the person who can achieve those things. It's about stepping into the potential you've always had but maybe haven't fully embraced.

Coach's Notes: Rachael's story highlights a pivotal moment where mindset shifts create action. Use her experience as a reminder that the first step toward growth often starts with conquering internal hesitation.

So, how do you unlock this power?

1. **Mindset Shift:** Start by shifting your mindset from "I'm doing okay" to "I'm capable of greatness." You have to believe it before you can achieve it.

2. **Set Bigger Goals:** Don't just aim for what you think is possible—aim for what you want, even if it feels out of reach. Stretch yourself.

3. **Action:** Start taking the actions that align with the person you want to become. If you want to be a top leader, start acting like one now, even if you're not there yet.

4. **Surround Yourself with Growth:** Spend time with people who push you to be better. The more you're around those who challenge you, the more you'll grow into that next-level version of yourself.

You weren't made to be average, and if you're here, you know that deep down. So, stop settling for what's comfortable and start pushing for what's possible. The power to be more is already within you—you just have to believe it, embrace it, and act on it. Your future self is waiting.

The Power To Believe

Alright, let's take a little trip down memory lane. Who here has a three-year-old, or at least remembers being around one? Let me tell you, three-year-olds are savage. They're powerful, assertive, and they don't care one bit if they offend you. Why? Because they believe in themselves, without question. But somewhere along the way, many of us lost that.

Remember when you were three? The world was a magical place full of endless possibilities. You believed in the tooth fairy, Santa Claus, and that you could be anything you wanted—an astronaut, a princess, the president.

Then one day, boom. Reality hit. You were told the tooth fairy isn't real, Santa doesn't exist, and "people like you" don't become astronauts or princesses. Over time, the power of that three-year-old— the power to believe—was stripped away. We weren't born with self-doubt; we learned it. But here's the good news; we can unlearn it. We can relearn how to believe in ourselves and our dreams.

I have a three year old who believes she can conquer the world. She's fearless and unapologetically herself. She embraces her dreams without hesitation. Watching her reminds me of the power of belief and how it shapes our reality. Belief is powerful. It's the foundation of success. Without belief, we limit ourselves and our potential.

The power to believe is not just something you had as a child—it's something you can reclaim. It's the foundation for everything you want to achieve in life and in this industry. When you believe in yourself, you become unstoppable. You start to take risks, to step out of your comfort zone, and to chase after your dreams with a fierceness you didn't know you had.

So, how do you start believing in yourself again?

1. **Reconnect with Your Inner Child:** Remember what it felt like to believe anything was possible. Tap into that energy and let it guide you.

2. **Positive Affirmations:** Speak life into your dreams. Use affirmations daily to remind yourself of your potential and power.

3. **Celebrate Wins:** Big or small, start celebrating your successes. Each win is proof that you're capable and that you're on the right path.

4. **Surround Yourself with Believers:** Spend time with people who believe in you, who see your potential and who will remind you of it when you start to doubt yourself. Their belief in you can help reignite your own.

You have the power to believe, and it's a power that can transform your life. It's time to shake off the doubts and start believing in yourself again—like that fearless three-year-old who knew they could be anything, because guess what? You can. So let's reclaim that power, let's believe in our dreams, and let's go out there and make them happen.

The Power To Dream

Let's play a game. Imagine you couldn't fail—how big would you dream? The only thing standing between you and your wildest dreams is, well, you. If you can dream it, you can achieve it. But it all starts with believing in the power of your dreams.

Your dreams are not just figments of your imagination. They are the blueprint to your success. The only thing stopping you from achieving them is you.

Dreams are powerful. They're the driving force behind every major achievement, every breakthrough, every leap of faith. But here's the thing—most people don't dream big enough. They let fear, doubt, and past failures shrink their dreams down to a size that feels "safe." But safe doesn't lead to greatness. If you want to be an incredible network marketer, you have to start by dreaming big and then taking steps every day to turn those dreams into reality.

Let me tell you about my kids. 2 of my daughters love to dance, and my son is into football. They started young, and they've spent years practicing, learning from pros, and honing their skills. The more time they spend in their dream, the more normal it becomes to them. They're comfortable on the stage, on the field, because they've immersed themselves in that environment. It's no longer a dream; it's becoming their reality.

But here's the challenge with network marketing—it often comes into our lives later, when we've already been conditioned to play it safe. We haven't spent enough time "in the dream" to feel like we belong there. But just like my kids, the more time you spend around people who are living your dream, the more familiar—and achievable—it becomes.

If you don't stay close to the fire, you'll never get comfortable with the heat. To turn your dreams into reality, you need to surround yourself with people who are already living the life you want, who have the paychecks, the freedom, and the success you aspire to. The more you immerse yourself in that environment, the more normal it will feel to you. And before you know it, you'll start to believe that your dreams aren't just possible—they're inevitable.

Here's how to start living in your dreams:

1. **Get Close to the Fire:** Attend every company event, every training, every meeting where you can connect with top leaders. Proximity is power.

2. **Touch Your Dreams:** Spend time around the people who are where you want to be. Whether it's through mentorship, networking, or just observing—immerse yourself in their world.

3. **Daily Steps:** Take one step every day that moves you closer to your dream. It could be learning a new skill, making a new contact, or simply visualizing your success.

4. **Believe You Belong:** The more time you spend in the world of your dreams, the more you'll start to feel like you belong there. And when you believe you belong, the universe has a funny way of making space for you.

Your dreams are powerful, and they're waiting for you to make them a reality. Don't let fear or doubt keep you from the life you deserve. Get close to the fire, touch your dreams, and take steps every day to turn them into your reality. The power of your dreams is within you—now go out there and make them happen

THE GIFT OF HOPE... To Help One Person Everyday

In network marketing, hope is your secret weapon. It's what drives you to keep pushing forward, even when the odds seem stacked against you. Hope is powerful because it's the spark that lights the fire of persistence, resilience, and ultimately, success.

There was a time in my journey when everything seemed to be falling apart. I was working hard, doing everything right, but the results just weren't coming. I felt like giving up, like maybe this wasn't for me. But deep down, I held on to a little glimmer of hope. I reminded myself why I started, what I was working toward, and what was possible if I just kept going. That hope was enough to get me through the tough days, to keep me moving forward when it felt easier to quit. Guess what? Things turned around. The results started to show, and all that hard work paid off. But it wouldn't have happened if I hadn't held on to hope.

Hope is powerful because it keeps you in the game long enough to see the results of your efforts. It's the anchor that holds you steady during the storms. Without hope, it's easy to give up, to walk away when things get tough. But with hope, you have the strength to keep going, to keep believing, and to keep pushing forward until you reach your goals.

So as we come to the end of this chapter, I want you to remember this: The power of you is real. It's not just a nice idea or a motivational phrase. It's the truth. You are unique, and that uniqueness is your superpower. You have the power to be more, to believe in yourself, to change your life, to dream big, to follow the blueprint, and to hold on to hope.

In network marketing, the most important asset you have is you. Your journey, your story, your dreams, and your determination—they are all part of the power of you. So, as you move forward, remember that you are powerful beyond measure. Embrace that power, use it to fuel your success, and never forget that you have everything you need within you to achieve greatness. Now, it's time to take action. Use the power of you to change your life and to make a difference in the

lives of others. Your journey is just beginning, and the possibilities are endless. You've got this—now go out there and show the world the power of you!

Coach's Notes: Belief is the cornerstone of all success. Reflect on where your belief system might be holding you back and what steps you can take to rebuild it stronger. Follow Rachael's incredible strategies and take massive action.

"If you have a smartphone and you're not making any money from it, it's not very smart is it?"

— Unknown

LEAH LOCKETT

- 50k social media followers across all platforms.

- Corporate real estate background until the age of thirty when I found my calling in the NWM industry with a travel based product.

- Sacked my boss fourteen months later after building a six figure income that is now multiple six and on track for seven.

- Has helped thousands of people globally within the industry and trained on stages across the world.

Stop Recruiting – start BUILDING

After just eleven short months in network marketing and with no previous experience, I had hit a rank up that almost guaranteed a six figure legacy income in my company, sacked my boss and retired myself from life as I knew it in corporate real estate at the age of 31.

Having never been in network marketing before, and not being the industry's biggest fan (but I'll come onto this later), at the time I didn't realise how big of a deal what I had done was. In fact I even struggled to duplicate what I had done for a while, because I wasn't really in tune with what I had done, or how I had done it.

So, I had to look at the way I had 'built' what I had, so that I could then teach what I knew, because good isn't good unless it's duplicatable right??

So when I got into it, and started to delve into the how and the why of my journey I noticed something, and it was the secret sauce to my success.

I have never recruited a single person to my business... I know what you're thinking, come on Leah, how have you become one of the top income earners in the business and have one of the fastest moving teams in the company... without recruiting?? It's simple really, and I am going to teach you everything you need to know.

I want you to stop recruiting – and to START BUILDING.

I am not and have never been in the recruitment business, and I think the problem I had with my view of network marketing previously was – I had seen people treating people like numbers, recruiting solely for the sake of ranks and income.

It was what put me off even having a look at working online in NWM for so many years previously – you see I used to be a network marketing hater and now I am a network marketing educator. I got to be the change I wanted to see in the industry and now I get to teach that, it wasn't the industry I disliked, it wasn't the life of freedom I didn't like and it certainly wasn't residual income I disliked... it was the desperation to bring people into the industry as a recruit and not a partner, so when I say I am not in the business of recruiting, what do I mean?

Well, I'm in the business of BUILDING; I build people, I build businesses, I build belief systems and confidence in others and something I do extremely well is build legacy incomes with people for themselves and their families.

So first, I'd like you to understand the fundamental differences between recruiting and building.

1. **What is the difference between recruiting your frontline & building a team?** Your frontline is the people you have personally brought in, and that is the foundation for you to build a team from, but it is not solely how you build a leveraged income via multi-levels.

2. **What is TEAM BUILDING?** Some of you know how to recruit – but you do not know how to BUILD a team! Team building is defined as the action or process of causing a group of people to work effectively towards a common goal, leveraged income!

3. This is why I have a TEAM of other people successful in their own right, who are leading their own teams within my organisation. But how is that I have done that, and how can you do the same? I pride myself on understanding and being the biggest fan of the beautiful industry we operate in, which means, I am able to effectively communicate my vision and subsequently duplicate it to thousands.

Some of you are terrified of leading with residual income and the opportunity we have at our fingertips with our model, and me... well I lead with it! So let me simplify it.

•   The first side of your model is selling a product or a service. Inevitably, there's commissions involved there, BUT that's not why we get involved in network marketing itself. We didn't get involved just for the one-off commissions of the sale.

- A true network marketing company – WITH A COMPENSATION PLAN LIKE YOURS, you joined more than likely because you wanted residual income. You wanted someday down the road, money coming in without you putting all the effort in to get it.

- It's called leverage. It's the beauty of our profession. It's becoming something that's less and less spoken about because it's connected to multi-level marketing, network marketing, as if that's a bad word... it isn't and when you understand the power of what you are doing, and more importantly WHY you are doing it.

You can start building people that will come in and build WITH YOU - YOU ARE SCARED OF THE RESIDUAL INCOME MODEL – AND I LEAD WITH IT.

So let me give you some tips on the do's and don'ts for switching your mindset from recruiting to building.

What *Not* To Do

- JOIN MY TEAM POSTS – you are recruiting people in as a number with no connection to their why or their goals, why are they doing this, how can this change their life, what does their version of success look like?

- Sending spammy and cold recruitment messages – This only happens when you are attached to the sale, you become needy – and guess what It shows, you have built no relationship, no trust and subsequently it becomes near impossible to build anything sustainable with this person.

What *To* Do

- Become a provider of a service and a solver of a problem – in order to do this effectively, you must learn to focus on the needs of your new business partner or prospect and learn to become detached from the outcome, if the model isn't for them – don't take it personally, there are plenty of people this is for! We are not in the business of convincing, we are in the business of sorting through who this is and who this isn't for!

- Selling your product or providing a service online doesn't have to be spammy, and we certainly don't need to convince or beg people to partner with us or buy from us. So stop thinking of people as a sale and start thinking of them as a human.

- A person will feel like a sale or a number, only when you barge into someone's dm's/phone/space with YOUR NEEDS instead of focusing on theirs. Want to shift your numbers? Then stop making it about you!

Now that we have covered the basics, something that really helps me to share my vision and create a relationship that enables me to duplicate effectively is understanding my business partner and THEIR needs over and above my own... This stage is done whilst I'm building the relationship and the rapport with them which can be prior to bringing them into the business or in the very early stages of onboarding in a critical conversation call where I find out what they would like from the business, and how I can subsequently help them to achieve this with our model.

Now I am not asking you to go around asking these questions to everyone you speak to, but having an understanding of your prospect or new business partner, and why THEY are here...really helps with my duplication process.

Below I have outlined some of the things I like to have an awareness of so that I can effectively coach someone through their business and towards their goals;

Getting to know your Prospect or New Business Partner

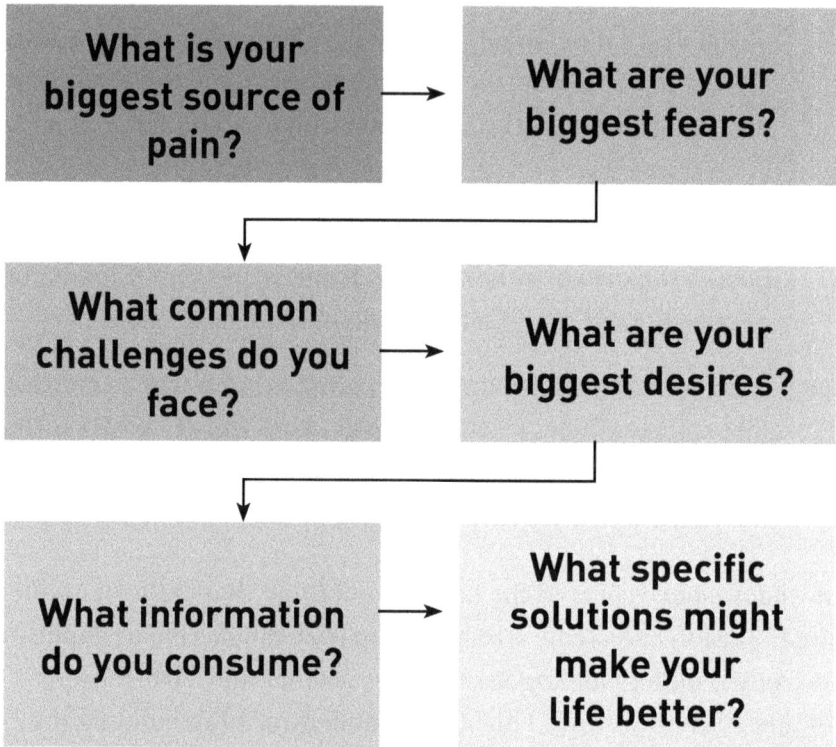

What is your biggest source of pain? →	**What are your biggest fears?**	

What common challenges do you face? →	**What are your biggest desires?**	

What information do you consume? →	**What specific solutions might make your life better?**	

If I think back to the time I first found the industry and answer the above questions in a past tense, **this very model that we have – gave me solutions and then some to every one of my pain points.**

My lack of time freedom, my desire for more income, the need to feel like I was able to make the rest of my life, the best of my life. Without knowing any of this about me it would have been really hard for me to catch a vision I couldn't see. So when speaking to people moving forwards, think about what you are offering, how powerful the vehicle is that we have and communicate it effectively, so that others can start to paint their own vision.

- Would you have been able to do this with a JOIN MY TEAM my team post?

- Or would you have been able to communicate this by getting to know me, showing me the comp plan, letting me look at the documentation of others, showing me that the model works and it is possible for me too?

Coach's Notes: What Leah shares here is transformative: shifting from a recruitment mindset to a building mindset isn't just a strategy—it's a philosophy. Building is about investing in people and creating relationships rooted in trust and shared goals. By focusing on your prospect's needs rather than your own, you create a foundation for lasting success. This isn't about hitting numbers; it's about helping people transform their lives. When you internalize this, everything changes—not just your results, but your entire approach to leadership and growth.

The 3 B's (Belief, Belief, Belief!!)

The work is important, mastering the mundane is important, long-term vision is important, but the pillars to being able to consistently apply these to your business to be able to get to the desired outcome you set out for, all stem from BELIEF.

Usually when coaching my team, I see lack of one of the 3 beliefs required to make it work in the industry, sometimes all 3 are lacking.

1. **Belief in the Network Marketing profession generally.**
   If you don't believe in the industry – educate yourself on what Network Marketing is and what Network Marketing isn't - Network Marketing is one of the most heavily regulated and professional industries in the world, it is also an industry on the rise!! With a current value of $211.55 Billion in 2023 with a 2030 forecast of $328.26 billion.

   The sooner you become a student of the profession and arm yourself with data and facts and figures, the easier it is to become an educator of what we do and why we are doing it.

Coach's Notes: Leah's emphasis on belief is profound. Without belief in the profession, your company, or yourself, you'll find it difficult to lead, inspire, or even act consistently. But here's the thing: belief isn't just a feeling—it's built through education, action, and surrounding yourself with success stories. Take this challenge: every day, focus on strengthening one of the three beliefs Leah outlines. Whether it's diving into network marketing's growth data, studying your company's success stories, or writing yourself a belief check, small actions compound to build unstoppable confidence.

2. **Belief in your company or product/service.**
   If you don't believe in your model or product/service - look around at the documentation of others and educate yourself over and over again on the success of others – leverage the stories and successes of others, whilst you continue to write your own success story. And remember, have a strong VISION whilst you write your success story – eventually your vision will become your story.

3. **Perhaps the most important; belief in yourself.**
    If you don't believe in yourself, the first step to knowing this is doable for you, and it is by the way it's doable for anyone!

    You see, our profession does not discriminate. It doesn't care your age, your gender, your political or religious views nor your education...it only cares what you do and WHO YOU HELP. The first step to gaining belief in yourself, is to look around, there are so many success stories of people less qualified than you, just because they believed in themselves and took action! Borrow your belief from someone else who's already where you want to be!

Coach's Notes: Borrowing belief from others until you find your own is one of the most powerful tools Leah shares here. Think of belief as a muscle: the more you work it, the stronger it gets. In the early days, when doubt creeps in, lean on the stories of those who've paved the way. Learn from their success, emulate their habits, and allow their journeys to fuel your confidence. Remember, belief isn't static—it grows with every step you take toward your vision.

The second step to this is to write yourself a belief cheque. Success loves speed in our industry the quicker you see this work for you, and the more often, the higher your belief system fills!! So make it your mission to start small and keep building not just your belief, but your relationships, your business and subsequently your bank balance....with belief cheques! Then help everyone attached to you to write their own.

"Coming together is a beginning. Keeping together is progress. Working together is success."

– Henry Ford, founder of Ford Motor Company

MILES & HEIDI STALLARD

- Individually multiple million dollar earners.

- Over $100 million in sales.

- Miles - International pastor.

- Heidi - Health coach, nutritionist and former fitness competitor.

Being Unstoppable as a Couple in Network Marketing

Building a business can be one of the most rewarding experiences of your life, but doing it as a couple brings its own set of opportunities... and challenges. Balancing a business the dynamics of marriage requires intentionality, communication, and teamwork.

When we started building our network marketing business together, we were excited about the possibilities but quickly learned that success wouldn't come without effort—not just in the business but in our relationship.

We've experienced the ups and downs of building a business as a couple. There were moments when emotions influenced business decisions, and times when reaching shared goals or going through challenges brought us closer than ever. Through trial and error, we've discovered strategies that not only strengthened our business partnership but also enhanced our marriage.

In this chapter, we share our journey—both the triumphs and trials—of building a network marketing business as a couple. You'll hear each of our perspectives and gain practical tips that have helped us succeed. Our hope is to inspire you with stories, insights, and actionable advice to create your own success story as a team.

Miles' Perspective

When I started network marketing, I was 24, working eighty hour weeks as an insurance claims adjuster, and earning a six-figure salary. But I wanted more freedom and control over my life. Network marketing seemed like the path to achieve that.

Convincing Heidi, my girlfriend at the time, was a different story. She thought focusing elsewhere was making a mistake. We were seriously dating and planning our future, but she didn't see the potential I saw and even discouraged my friends from joining.

While she left to do the summer study abroad program, I got to work! I doubled down on building my business and reached milestones quickly, including qualifying for a car bonus. When I shared the news with her, it turned out she had also experienced her own realization while overseas. She began to see that her current path might not offer the life she truly wanted.

When she returned, we both decided to build our businesses separately at first, which allowed us to find our own rhythm. Within a year, we each hit six-figure positions before getting married and then transitioned to working as a team.

Working together wasn't always easy. We often disagreed on strategies, and business issues occasionally spilled into our personal life. But through communication and a willingness to adapt, we found a balance. Now, as parents and top leaders, we've built a life of freedom—together.

Heidi's Perspective

When Miles first brought up network marketing, I was skeptical. So skeptical that I thought he was crazy! He had a six-figure job, and I couldn't understand why he would risk it.

At the time he was doing well and I was focused on finishing school in the day, while making six figures bartending nights at a high-volume sports bar and one of the top clubs in the nation. I didn't see network marketing as a real solution... until I did.

I was in China on a short school program when I began to question my own future.

In the quiet time I had with no one to talk to I looked inward and came face to face with the reality I wasn't willing to accept- I was going to graduate with my degree and make less money than I was making bartending.

I was desperate to get out of the service industry lifestyle as it was hard on my body and felt like a moral problem the longer I was there. So, naturally, I decided to drop online classes, had a panic attack and knew I needed to buy myself more time to figure out a plan.

I cried out to God for a solution... and he sure does have a funny (and humbling) way of delivering answers. The next day, before I could share that I dropped my classes Miles called to share his success, and it clicked for me—If he could do what he did working his hours then why couldn't I?

When I returned, I dove into building my own business since we were only dating but as young adults it also allowed us to grow individually before merging our efforts.

In the beginning, Miles excelled in structure and analytics, while I focused on relationships. We clashed at times but learned to leverage our strengths and complement each other. We had to figure out along the way how to approach the business as a team. Through the years, we have developed a good ebb and flow in and out of different areas together.

Nine years later, network marketing has given us the flexibility to be present with each other, our daughter, and the opportunity to travel all around experiencing life and making memories together.

Practical Tips for Couples in Network Marketing: Stories and Strategies

Communication and Appreciation Over Expectation

When we first started building separately, we had vastly different building styles. Chances are if you're building with a significant other you do, too. The goal is to realize *YOU'RE ON THE SAME TEAM* and how to use this to your advantage.

One of you might love detailed discussions about goals, strategies, and analytics, while the other is all about big-picture dreaming.

One of you might have a detailed plan for a presentation or training, but the other wants to "wing it."

Instead of focusing on where the other person lacks (in your opinion), sit down and talk about each other's strengths; and appreciate what each other brings to the table not only as a partner, but a business partner. Then make it a priority to do regular check-ins where you openly share challenges and wins, ensuring that you stay aligned working towards the same goal in your own way. Just don't forget to take time to edify one another, to each other.

Coach's Notes: Miles and Heidi's story gives a great balance of individuality and teamwork that's vital for couples in network marketing. Whether you're defining roles, adjusting to life changes, or learning to stay in your lane, the key is appreciating the strengths your partner brings to the table. The magic happens when you're not just building a business, but building each other. Take a moment to reflect: How can you better support your partner's strengths while pursuing your shared vision?

Stay in Your Lane

When our daughter was born, we realized our dynamic had to shift. Miles took the lead on building and traveling, while I focused on a new season and doing things online to help train and grow our team. We had to communicate and define our roles so we could play to our strengths in that season. But through the season of life changes it's important to define and redefine your roles so you can.

Defining clear roles not only reduced stress but also strengthened our trust in each other's capabilities and knows when we are veering off into the other's lane.

Wherever you are, be there

Early on and in our younger years, we were so focused on hitting our goals that work bled into every part of our lives. Date nights just turned into extra enjoyable business meetings. But as we had our daughter, we realized how easy it is to miss out on milestone moments with each other or your family because you're taking calls and responding to messages with no limits.

In order to maintain healthy business and family dynamics and most importantly, avoid burnout, it's not only more fulfilling but NECESSARY to set boundaries with technology and teams; especially during high-pressure months. So set guilt-free boundaries you both can adhere to on a regular basis with the understanding that every now and then you may have to adjust. Then, whenever you exercise a boundary, you know it's for the purpose of pursuing something greater, personally and professionally.

Be Patient During Growth

There have been seasons where one of us felt "stuck" while the other was thriving. During my postpartum recovery, Miles stepped up to cover more of the workload without making me feel guilty. But when things shifted later in business, it was my turn to carry the team. The benefit of building together is that when life happens, like the grief of losing a loved one, a health hiccup, or pursuing another passion, you have each other.

It's important to remember you have each other and that seasons come and go. Communicate and compromise on what season each of you are going through and extend grace and patience, instead of expectation and resentment.

Business growth isn't always linear and neither is personal growth. Once you recognize that you may blossom in different seasons, it makes things much easier. It's a marathon, not a sprint—and having someone in your corner makes all the difference.

Coach's Notes: One of the most powerful lessons in this chapter is learning to embrace the different seasons of growth, both in your business and personal life. As Heidi mentions, patience and grace during these times create the space for mutual support. This isn't just a business tip—it's a relationship superpower. Next time you feel "out of sync" with your partner, ask yourself: How can I meet them where they are and support them in this season?

When those aligned seasons come together, you both can enjoy the magic because you know what it takes to always have each other's back.

Create a Shared Vision

Our shared vision has always been the driving force behind our success, but it wasn't perfectly aligned from the start. When we began building our business while dating, we each had individual goals. As we grew together in marriage, we worked to combine those goals into a unified vision that reflected both of our dreams. Revisiting this vision regularly during team retreats and personal goal-setting sessions has kept us grounded and motivated, especially during challenging times. A shared vision is like a compass you can point each other back to—it keeps you focused and guides you back on track when life feels overwhelming.

At the same time, flexibility is essential. Life has a way of throwing unexpected challenges, and staying rigid can make things harder. We've learned to adapt when circumstances change, adjusting roles, timelines, or approaches while keeping our vision in sight. It's the balance between holding onto your vision while also making sure to be flexible on how it gets done that makes the journey both productive and fulfilling.

Coach's Notes: A shared vision is like the glue that binds a partnership, especially in a dynamic industry like network marketing. As Miles and Heidi demonstrate, revisiting your goals together isn't just about staying aligned—it's about rediscovering your "why" during every season. This shared vision not only keeps you grounded but serves as a reminder of what you're building toward, even when life throws challenges your way. For couples building together, when was the last time you revisited your vision together?

Your Call to Action

Start implementing one or two of these tips today. Schedule a check-in with your partner to discuss your goals and challenges, and take time to celebrate the things you've accomplished together!

Building a network marketing business as a couple is a beautiful, messy, and rewarding journey. It's not just about financial success but about growing together, playing to your strengths, and creating a life that reflects your shared dreams. By embracing the process with communication, trust, and teamwork, you can achieve *unstoppable success* and build something truly extraordinary—together.

"Success doesn't happen overnight but success comes from the small things that are done consistently over time."

– Lenika Scott

GREGG & DR. LENIKA SCOTT

- 8 Figure income earners & servant leaders.

- Millions in Real Estate secured "Debt Free" due to MLM.

- 2023 Worldwide #1 Power Rankers in current company.

- Over 1 Million reps in largest organization built to date.

- Highest Month in the industry: **1 Million** dollars in commissions.

Coach's Notes: Gregg and Lenika's story isn't just about numbers or houses—it's an example to how discipline, vision, and faith can turn seemingly impossible dreams into reality. As you read this, take a moment to reflect on the financial freedom you want for yourself and your family. What habits, mindsets, or decisions need to shift for you to reach that place?

Get Out Of Debt - Be Wise With Your Money

We just received the keys to our 2.6 MILLION DOLLAR, CUSTOM BUILT HOME, paid for in cash! Did you hear me? ALL CASH!

Our custom home has seven bedrooms, nine bathrooms, three kitchens and a beautiful pool. The home sits on eight acres of land with a creek that runs through the back of the property line. We are still in awe. We often have to pinch ourselves asking, is this real? Is this our life? God blessed us six years ago with a half a million dollar home paid for in cash.

We felt the Lord's heart was smiling and His desire for His children to pay the entirety of their homes. And do so in cash. As we traveled the world sharing our breakthrough testimony, so many lives were changed. Hope had been imparted and others were seeing that moving into a home **"Debt Free"** was possible. We'd soon start hearing others say we encouraged them to pay off their mortgage too.

Debt freedom had alway been in the forefront of our minds dating back 20+ years ago when we were just getting married. From using our tax returns on paying off vehicles to using inheritance checks to paying off debt, Gregg and I would often use extra income received to apply to debt we had accumulated. It became a habit and it became a way of life.

It however didn't come without a **FIGHT**. We had to endure bankruptcy, foreclose, be on food stamps over the course of years while we'd built our way to the top of two Network Marketing companies. There were many victories but there were many seasons of NOTHING. Meaning, it didn't look like a harvest based upon the seeds we had sown into people, our leaders and our team. It was because of this that we thought it would be beneficial to include that powerful victory of our personal journey within this chapter. We also thought it would be wise to share this...it is *imperative* you make smart decisions as you are building and growing your MLM business. We've seen people start building in this industry and lose it all due to terrible financial decisions or mismanaged seasons. If we could help just one leader in this industry by laying out our debt free simple formula it would be a great reward for us. Now let's review some "Debt Freedom" teaching that we live by.

Debt definition: Something owed. An OBLIGATION. A state of being under obligation to pay or repay someone or something in return for something received.

Did you know that mortgage means death grip in latin?

Debt is slavery. When you are in debt you are a slave which means you are entrapped and in bondage.

Some Debt Statistics

1. At least 8 out of 10 U.S. households are in debt.
According to a report by the Pew Charitable Trust, at least 80% of all U.S. households hold some sort of debt balance these days.

2. Our consumer debt has hit an all-time high of nearly $14 trillion.
Add up our mortgages, credit cards, student loans, car loans, personal loans, payday loans, and other lines of credit, and we now owe about $14 trillion as a nation.

3. We have FAR more debt than savings.
Studies show that keeping an emergency savings fund is vital for financial stability and wellbeing, but about half of all Americans couldn't even come up with $400 today in case of an emergency without selling something, borrowing, or taking on more harmful debt!

admin. "5 Shocking Statistics about Debt - Roundleaf Inc." Roundleaf Inc - Debt Consolidation and Settlement Company, 14 Feb. 2019, www.roundleafinc.com/5-shocking-statistics-about-debt/. Accessed 17 Nov. 2024.

Spiritual Bullets on Debt

1. Debt is slavery

Debt is bondage. Debt is oppressive and it holds us in captivity. The lender controls your quality of life. The lender makes you their servant. Each month you have to take a portion of your income and apply it towards debt. Debt cripples your ability and causes you to have to put off things you would be able to do. It causes stress and affects your ability to be creative. When we are stressed, our creative ability is diminished. It holds us captive to a system that works against us and a system that is not for us.

2. Debt is part of the curse

Deuteronomy 28:43 They will lend to you, but you will not lend to them. They will be the head, but you will be the tail. All these curses will come on you. They will pursue you and overtake you until you are destroyed, because you did not obey the Lord your God and observe the commands and decrees he gave you. The will of God for our lives is for us to have dominion.

3. God wants to deliver you from Debt

Just as He delivered the "Widow with oil" in the bible, it is the will of the Father to deliver you!

Our motto: "Don't STARVE your way out, GROW your way out!"

As the checks start coming in, be wise and fruitful about your earnings. Keep building your income and while it is building make the decision to knock the debt out!

Coach's Notes: This framework isn't just about eliminating debt—it's about building a foundation for lasting financial security. Use these steps as a lens to evaluate your current financial habits. Think about

which step might be your greatest opportunity for growth: discipline, education, belief, or triumph.

The D.E.B.T. Formula

This is my husband and I unique formula that we have applied to our finances several times before earning millions:

D- **Discipline** (*Standards of Behavior + Vision + Consistency = Discipline*)

E- **Educate** (*Learn more about money and how to use it*)

B- **Belief** (*What are your beliefs about money? What is your "Money Story"?*)

T- **Triumph** (*Celebrate your WINS in the process to debt freedom*)

This is a very unique framework that Gregg and I have established. You will not see it on Google, YouTube or anywhere, unless you see it come from Gregg and I. There are five steps to the framework. Keep in mind, this is a high level view.

Step number one is all about the <u>prep work</u>. This is where you gather all of your finances and your financial information. Clarity is needed and you understand where you are currently at. Be honest with yourself and tell the truth. The prep work will take some time so don't rush through this process.

Step number two is all about discipline. **D is for Discipline.** Of course, anything in life where success and productivity is the end goal discipline is required. This includes getting out of debt. Small consistent habits can yield huge results. You must be disciplined to stay the course in your debt free journey. In order for change to occur, you must commit to self-discipline.

Step number three is all about education. **E is for Educate.** This section will highlight financial information and debt statistics in addition to educating you in understanding the importance of why you are the way that you are in turns to in terms of your relationship with money. Oftentimes we typically perform habits, or do things not even recognizing or realizing why we're doing it. Most of the financial decisions we make today dates back to childhood. Education is not just about statistics, numbers and data. But educating and learning why it is that you are believing the way that you are believing. Understanding past and current money habits is a part of the process.

Step number four is all about belief. **B is for Believe.** Why are you believing the way that you're believing? Do you believe that you can really get out of debt and live a life of financial freedom and abundance? Do you believe debt freedom is for you? One thing we often tell our clients is this, "Wealth is your birthright." You have a right to live a life of abundance and also natural freedom without stress or strain constantly worrying about your finances.

Step number five is all about triumph. **T is for Triumph.** It is all about your wins. There is victory. You reading this lets me know you are serious about triumphing over debt, and we want to let you know that it is possible. Yes! You can get out of debt, stay out of debt and change your financial future.

D.E.B.T.

These are steps that we took over the years. This isn't something that we just did one time, but we did several times, therefore we know it can work and that it is so possible. You know, one of the things about getting out of debt is putting in the work and also facing the truth. Being aware and facing the reality of where you are at no matter how difficult it may be.

We truly believe that financial freedom is for everyone! But even so, it is encouraged to always live within your means. Truth is, if looking at the financial situations, many people live beyond their means and especially those who've never experienced the five figure checks this industry often brings. Some people simply don't take the time to reflect on the difference between their wants and needs. Also, remember that *how* you pay your debt, bills, and others you owe has much to do with your character! One of the main principles of getting out of debt is honoring your word. Pay people back!

It is about your level of consistency that ultimately contributes to paving your way out of debt.

Where are you?
Above Water: Able to save and invest in debt freedom.
Sea Level: Have just enough to maintain.
Drowning: Have more *month* than *money*!

Develop Healthy Habits

Remember that it's not about how much money you make, it's about how much you keep and you are wise with. There's a balance to it all. Create wealth-keeping habits of stewardship and financial responsibility on your path to debt freedom.

In life, achieving small wins releases confidence and creates healthy habits. As you develop healthy habits even as your income grows and you are catapulted into financial increase, the habits will remain!

"You have been faithful over a few things, I will make you ruler over many things." — Matthew 25:23

Create Quick Wins

Focusing on paying off one debt at a time allows you to create quick wins. As you go along, your wins will cause you to be more apt to push and knock out even more debt! These wins become addictive and are so freeing!

Consistency is Everything

Most of the millionaires you see, meet, or hear about are first-generation millionaires. In other words, their wealth has not been handed down or inherited.

80% of millionaires are first-generational. Success is created in the things of the mundane. It is often the very things that the average person doesn't want to do that millionaires have done over and over again!

What this tells us is that it's all about:

- Following very simple habits and principles
- Making choices and the right decisions
- Maintaining consistency

Coach's Notes:: Consistency is the secret ingredient to any success story. It's not about how fast you go but about staying the course. Let Gregg and Lenika's journey remind you that debt freedom isn't just financial—it's emotional and spiritual freedom too. It all connects!

Whether it takes six months a year or even two years to clear your debt, it's all about staying with it. Breakthrough and results come when you bring things to completion. As you walk through your journey to debt freedom, let consistency and finishing strong be the underlying message!

Debt freedom is all about relieving yourself of stresses that you really don't have to deal with in life. Even during feelings of overwhelm, maintain consistency and stick to the plan of your debt free journey!

Withhold not good from them to whom it is due,
when it is in the power of thine hand to do it.
— Proverbs 3:27

"You don't need to be great to start , but you need to start ... if you want to become great."

– Zig Ziglar

GIORDANO CARRETTA

- International speaker.

- Went from bus boy with 30k in debt to top %1 in the company.

- Helped hundreds of people hit the top rank in the company.

- Spoke on stage at Go Pro (Eric Worre).

The 3-Step Formula to Recruit Influential People

You don't need to be the best on your team to make the most money. This is a powerful truth that many aspiring network marketers overlook. Imagine for a moment how your business would transform if you could recruit individuals who are more influential, skilled, and connected than you. The potential is staggering.

Coach's Notes: Success leaves clues, and Giordano's story is proof that it's not where you start but where you're willing to go. His transformation is an incredible example of what's possible when strategy meets determination.

I'm Giordano Carretta, and over the past decade in network marketing, I've gone from a busboy and soccer coach, burdened with $30,000 in debt, to ranking among the top 1% of my company. How did I do this? By mastering a three-step formula—one that not only revolutionized my career but also helped countless others achieve financial freedom.

In this chapter, I'm going to share that formula with you. This isn't just about finding recruits; it's about transforming your business and elevating your game. One of these steps is something that nobody else is teaching, and it could be the key to your success.

Step 1: Identify Your Ideal Business Partner

The first step in this transformative journey is to be incredibly specific about who you want to recruit. Think beyond mere demographics. Your ideal business partner should encompass traits, skills, and qualities that complement your vision.

Things to Consider:
1. **Skill Set:** What skills does this person need to have? Are they a great salesperson, a skilled networker, or perhaps a social media guru? Define these attributes clearly.
2. **Influence:** Look for individuals who already have a following or a reputation in their field. These are people who can amplify your message and bring new prospects into your network.
3. **Values and Vision:** Make sure their values align with yours. If you're passionate about personal development, find someone

who shares that passion. This alignment fosters a positive
working relationship.

4. **Motivation:** Identify what drives them. Are they motivated by
financial freedom, personal growth, or community impact?
Understanding their motivations will help you present your
opportunity in a way that resonates with them.

Actionable Tip:
Create a detailed profile of your ideal business partner. Include their
current job, interests, and how they could potentially fit into your
organization. The clearer you are, the easier it will be to spot these
individuals in your network.

**Coach's Notes: Clarity is the foundation of leadership.
When you know exactly who you're looking for, the
universe has a funny way of bringing them into your
orbit. Focus, and watch the magic happen.**

Step 2: Who Do I Need to Become?

Once you've identified your ideal business partner, it's time for some
introspection. What do you need to change about yourself to attract
these high-caliber individuals? This is about reverse engineering the
recruitment process.

Reflect on the Following:
1. **Skills Development:** Do you need to enhance your communication
skills, sales techniques, or product knowledge? Make a list of the
skills you need to develop and begin to work on them.
2. **Mindset Shift:** It's crucial to adopt a mindset of abundance.
Understand that just because someone is more influential
doesn't mean they're out of your reach. Believe in your value
and the opportunity you're offering.

3. **Networking and Presence:** Are you actively engaging in spaces where your ideal recruits hang out? Attend workshops, webinars, or networking events that align with their interests.

Actionable Tip:
Set a timeline for your personal development. Identify one skill you want to master over the next month and dedicate time each week to that pursuit.

Step 3: Change

The final step is perhaps the most difficult but also the most rewarding. For things to change in your business, YOU must change first. This is a long-term process, and it requires commitment and consistency.

Embrace the Journey:
1. Consistency is Key: Change doesn't happen overnight. Commit to your personal development and the recruitment process over the long haul. Celebrate small wins along the way.
2. Feedback Loop: Seek feedback from your team and mentors. Are there areas where you can improve? Constructive criticism can be invaluable.
3. Stay Open to Learning: The industry is constantly evolving. Stay updated on trends, tools, and strategies.

The Power of Change

Let me share a story about my first top recruit, Arturo. When I first met him, he was far more experienced and influential in his field than I was. He had a thriving career and a vast network. I remembered feeling intimidated but also inspired.

Instead of letting my insecurities hold me back, I focused on what I needed to learn and how I could add value to Arturo's life. I approached him with a clear proposition, emphasizing how he could leverage our network marketing opportunity to enhance his success.

To my surprise, he was intrigued. We connected deeply over shared values and visions. Today, Arturo is responsible for half of my entire organization, proving that recruiting someone more influential can exponentially grow your business.

Coach's Notes: Giordano's story about Arturo highlights a critical principle: value attracts value. When you lead with confidence and clear vision, even the most influential people will see the opportunity.

The Transformative Power of Your Network

Recruiting people who are more influential than you is not just a dream; it's a strategy that can take your business to unprecedented heights. By following this three-step formula—identifying your ideal business partner, reverse engineering who you need to become, and embracing the process of change—you'll position yourself to attract top talent.

Remember, it's a journey that requires patience and dedication. The right people are out there waiting for someone like you to lead them. Now go out there and transform your network marketing business!

"*You can't fight the waves,*
but you can learn how to surf."

– Jon Kabat

AMBER GUSTOWSKI

- Ten years in NWM profession.

- Heart led seven-figure earner.

- Top 1% of the company.

- Top three company earner.

- Helped create thousands of 4 and 5 figure earners.

Building Through Adversity and Adjusting Your Crown

What if I told you that your most painful challenges could be the key to actually unlocking your greatest power? I know you're probably sitting there and just rolled your eyes, I did too when I'd read truth-bombs like this, especially when I was in the thick of it. I'd think to myself "So you're saying that the adversity I'm facing isn't here to break me—but to BUILD me?!" I didn't want to believe this, I'd rather stay cozy in my pity party blanket fort. I spent years doubting myself, my worth, and whether I even had what it took to succeed in life, let alone network marketing! But as I look back now, I realize that everything I went through was preparing me for this beautiful journey of abundance, and I know in my heart it's possible for you too.

Coach's Notes: Amber's story shows that challenges aren't barriers—they're bridges. Use your hardships as stepping stones to build the life you've always envisioned.

Let's be honest, we all go through seasons of hardship and life definitely doesn't stop when you start building your business; if anything it tests you even more! To this day I am still juggling this, but one thing I've learned over the years is that you can't fight the waves but you can learn how to surf, and in the end that brings me so much peace every single time. I get it, the pressure of running a network marketing business while balancing family, bills, and your personal life can feel more like walking through fire. I truly believe it's in that fire that you are forged into the leader you're meant to be, and then you're truly unstoppable!

I wasn't born with a silver spoon, nor was I raised in an environment that encouraged me to dream big. In fact, I was born into child and family services with my fifteen year old Mom, living in over thirty seven homes and enduring a childhood of confusion, emotional and mental abuse that left me questioning whether I was ever enough, or if I'd ever feel safe or truly loved. Did I even trust myself?

Those scars stayed with me for years, they still creep up. They made me believe that success was for other people—people who had better upbringings, who were smarter, wealthier, or more capable than me. I didn't realize how much shame I felt just for being ME. I carried that belief into my adulthood and I didn't really have big dreams because I was too busy living in survival mode.

I was a young mom who was waitressing long nights just to scrape by, my husband was working overtime and we rarely saw each other with our schedules. I was exhausted, depressed, full of Mom guilt and our marriage was hurting. The weight of our financial struggles felt like this huge anchor pulling me down and I felt so unsafe. Despite this, I was determined to be the best Mom and woman I could be for my three babies; I desperately wanted to give them a life of security, blessings and possibility. I wanted to be an example of a powerful and loving woman to my daughter, to show her mountains can be moved and she can too! It was in those 3AM moments, lying in bed wide awake, heart pounding when I knew something had to change. I was determined to go from broke(n) to blessed, and from burnt out to burning bright! It was in those moments where I found my "why" and the strength to get through anything and it burned deep in my heart. There was a light inside me, I just needed the courage to turn it on.

In the middle of this crazy storm is actually when I found network marketing— I immediately saw possibility and it gave me hope and butterflies in my tummy. You mean I can stay home with my kids wearing my leggings and slippers and make money?! As in, uncapped earning potential?! Did you just say residual income?? You mean I can actually start to feel better and help other people too?! I was all in, and so I became a student in my first company and earned while I learned, It was pretty cool.

Family and friends doubted and questioned me, but I quickly learned they weren't the ones paying my bills, fixing my credit score, or giving me more quality time and experiences with my three babies and husband. I learned that people will talk behind your back no matter how kind or successful you are, it's always a sting to the heart but there's a reason why they are behind you and you deserve to stay laser focussed! Trust me, it's all worth it for the peace of mind, quality time with your loved ones, financial freedom, time freedom, and a chance to rewrite your story.

Believe me when I say that this now confident, seven figure earner who sits at the top 1% of her company's transformation didn't come instantly or easily. I played this "pity party adversity game" for over eight years in my Network Marketing career, and that was way too long! Although I was strong and had great leadership skills, built big teams and was great with people, when tough times came I really struggled. I learned a ton, I made money and memories, and there were also inevitable failures, pivots and changes along the way that would set me back way more than I should have let them. But what I had that set me apart from the 99%, was a deep hunger to make this profession work, that burnt deep within my heart.

In the end what it really came down to was relentless, confident, postured action day in and day out, topped with relentless belief in myself and what I had in my hands. My mindset was everything, the victim blame game mentality had to go. I did this day in and day out, and I started to see the light. In those moments of doubt, stress, and even failure, I found my power, it was hiding deep in my belly and it burned in my heart...I knew I just had to trust and keep taking action. I actually remember looking at myself in the mirror three years ago and saying out loud like a crazy person "Amber, you are where you ARE and are NOT in your life because of you...nobody else. Are you finally going to start playing big?! You know what to do." In that moment of full accountability with myself the game changed...I changed. I discovered that adversity isn't something to fear—it's something to embrace. It's what allows you to stand tall in the face of anything that comes your way in your network marketing business, and to keep moving forward, because you're worth it.

Coach's Notes: Accountability is the ultimate difference maker. When you take ownership of your results, you reclaim your power to create the future you desire.

So, if you don't already know, adversity is a given...but so is finding your power. Whether it's in your business, personal struggles, financial difficulties, or doubts from those around you, you'll face hard times. But it's in those moments where you have the opportunity to rise up and remember who you are! Remember why you are doing this and turn your light all the way up! I started to change all my WTF (what the fudge) thoughts into WIT (whatever it takes) thoughts and everything started to shift. It felt lighter, more empowering. Try it!

In my one on one coaching sessions, one of the most common things that come up is self-doubt and a poor mindset. It's easy to feel overwhelmed when the obstacles stack up—when you're juggling a million responsibilities, facing rejection, or dealing with personal issues. These moments can make you question everything: Is this worth it? Do I have what it takes? Why is this so hard? It's a terrible feeling! In those dark moments, it's easy to let fear win and to let it convince you that you're not enough, but the truth is adversity is only as powerful as the story you tell yourself about it. Remember, it's not here to BREAK you, but to BUILD you and you are simply learning how to surf the waves! Every time a negative story creeps up, I simply say out loud "clear, cancel, delete" and I choose the next highest thought. It works every time.

I want to give you some of my superpowers that I've found over the years that help me build my network marketing business through the hard times. They help me readjust my crown, find my personal power, and push through when it feels impossible:

1. Remember who you are deep in your heart. If your intentions are good and your heart is pure, you'll find your way.

2. Your "why" is the anchor that will keep you grounded when the storms hit. Let your "why" give you a burn deep within your beautiful soul. On days when I didn't want to show up, I reminded myself why I started. You need to do the same. Write down your why. Visualize it. Let it fuel you when the road gets rough.

3. Tap into your personal power. Adversity has a way of clouding your vision and making you forget who we really are. You are powerful. You are worthy of success. You are unbreakable! Don't let fear and doubt rob you of your potential. Every challenge you face is an opportunity to tap into your strength and prove to yourself what you're capable of. Adjust your crown and keep moving!

4. Give yourself grace, and don't give up. Take accountability, then turn your self-loathing into self-love and self-belief! There will be days when it feels like everything and everyone is against you. In those moments, give yourself grace. It's okay to feel overwhelmed. It's okay to struggle. But don't let that be the reason you quit. Keep moving forward, even if it's just one small step at a time.

5. You can't fight the waves but you can learn how to surf. After a while it gets easier and easier, and before you know it even the big waves don't frighten you, instead they excite you.

6. Turn your WTF (what the fudge) moments into WIT (whatever it takes) moments...Start doing this and your game will change.

7. Clear, Cancel, Delete...Choose the next highest thought.

8. Trust the process while taking relentless action.

Coach's Notes: Adversity reveals your inner strength. Amber's practical tips are more than strategies— they're lifelines to keep you grounded and growing through life's toughest seasons. I have the opportunity to personally work with Amber and watch her consistently crush her business.

In the end, I hope the thought of building through adversity no longer makes you want to crawl into the fetal position and hide in your blanket for drinking slurpees (can you tell I'm Canadian) for seven days straight. It is simply a part of life, and it doesn't have to completely define you. Instead, let it be your guiding light. Let it be the thing that builds you into the leader, the entrepreneur, the parent and the person you're meant to be. When you face challenges, remind yourself of your why, tap into your power, adjust your crown and keep pushing forward.

You have the power within you to build a life of freedom, abundance, and purpose. None of this is negotiable or up for debate. I know this because I've lived it. I can be unstoppable, so can you.

"Life is living both tragically and magically simultaneously, where heartache and joy walk hand in hand, teaching us that beauty often grows in the cracks of our brokenness."

— Robin Hodges

ROBIN HODGES (ROWDEN)

- Achieved multiple six-figure earnings annually over several years.

- Successfully led a team of 17,000+ people.

- Attained top-tier ranks in four separate companies.

- Raised a child with severe medical issues while excelling professionally.

- Overcame the profound impact of sudden personal loss.

Out of the Ashes: Rebuilding Life After Tragedy

Welcome to the Thunderdome. That's how it feels to me. Welcome to one of the most emotional, most challenging journeys you'll ever embark on to become successful. You're in for the ride of your life.

You might think we've had it easy, that everything just fell into place. We met Rob, followed his lead, and everything magically worked out. Maybe you imagine us living in big homes, driving fancy cars, and enjoying perfect marriages. Perhaps you think our lives are the picture-perfect moments you see on social media, that we don't understand real struggle, that we've never faced what you're going through.

But you couldn't be more wrong.

What if I told you that some of us experienced profound personal violations and trauma at a young age? That some endured unimaginable pain, facing harm that left deep physical and emotional scars. What if I told you that was only the beginning of our story?

What if I told you that some of us have watched our only child suffer through severe epilepsy—so severe that two brain surgeries were required, surgeries that left her unable to use her right side for ten long months?

What if I told you that the same person then woke up one morning to find the man she thought she would marry had suddenly died just thirty minutes after waking up, six days before their seven-year anniversary, and twenty days before her birthday?

Would you think we've had it easy as we speak from stages? Would you still judge us, trash talk those you see sitting high on the MLM food chain without knowing the battles we've faced? Or would you start to see us as human beings who have had to overcome more than you could ever imagine?

Coach's Notes: I have watched Robin's growth for many years. If you knew her even just 5 years ago you wouldn't recognize her because her growth has been beyond incredible. Robin's honesty reminds us that every leader has a backstory. Empathy and understanding are essential as you rise in your own journey—never assume you know someone's full story.

These are just some of the challenges I've faced. My life has been a fight for survival, a war against anyone who stood in my way.

However, tragedy, despair, and pain—if you let them—have a way of transforming you for the better.

Let's start by saying: I DID IT ALL WRONG at the beginning of my career. I didn't always do things right. I burned bridges, tore down my own empires, and severed ties with people who loved me and helped me achieve my dreams. There was a point when I was ready to turn my back on this entire industry, leaving nothing but destruction in my wake. I thought I was telling it like it is, but all I was really doing was causing harm.

The higher I climbed, the harder I fell. I lived my life angry—furious at everyone around me. I was not coachable. In fact, I was the worst person to have on your team. I was a mess—a complete disaster, and not the beautiful kind Beyoncé sings about.

Losing someone so suddenly stripped me of everything—mentally, physically, and emotionally. The pain forced me to become someone I had never been before. It softened me. It made me see the world, people, and circumstances through a different lens.

Coach's Notes: True transformation often comes through pain. Robin's journey teaches us that vulnerability can become your greatest strength when you channel it toward growth.

After sitting with his body for nearly four hours, I finally left. I shut the door behind me and cried harder than I ever had in my entire life. At that moment, I made a promise to God and the Universe that I would be kind. I vowed that I would always cherish people and never allow anger or rage to dictate my life again.

I went home that day and stayed there, not stepping outside for three and a half months.

In those moments of silence, I sat with my grief, feeling every bit of it. I was lost and numb, unsure of how I would rebuild a life that I was now forced to reconstruct from the ground up. I just sat there—empty, sad, angry—and more than anything, I felt an overwhelming guilt that he had passed without me saying sorry or goodbye.

After almost four months of isolating myself at home, a good friend called and asked me to visit him in Utah. Desperately needing to escape everything and everyone that reminded me of my pain, I quickly boarded a plane to Salt Lake City. That trip would forever change how I viewed the direct sales industry.

When I arrived, I learned that my friend, who had started his own company just six months earlier, was hosting their very first American event. He assured me I didn't have to attend; he just wanted me to get out of the house, to be with him and his family. Even though I had absolutely no intention of attending the event, I found out that Rob Sperry, the first coach I ever connected with, was going to be the keynote speaker. Seeing Rob again felt like a small spark of excitement in the midst of my sorrow.

During my time there, I ended up attending more than just that event. I went to Top Leader dinners, gatherings, trainings, ribbon cuttings, and celebrations. The leaders were from every corner of the globe, most of them speaking languages I didn't understand.

But what struck me most was their excitement—the pure, unfiltered happiness I could feel in their energy. I remember thinking that it was the first time I'd felt happiness since the tragedy I had experienced. It was incredible to witness such joy, drive, and determination in others.

I overheard one of the owners quoting Jim Rohn: "We generally change ourselves for one of two reasons: inspiration or desperation."

In that moment, tears welled up in my eyes as I realized just how inspired I was by these people from all over the world. For the first time in my career, I wasn't driven by desperation. I wasn't angry. I wasn't desperately chasing money or ranks. I was simply inspired—by the people and the industry I had once thrown away.

I made a decision that day: I was going to step back into the MLM space, but this time as a different person with a new perspective. This time, I allowed myself to trust and to be vulnerable. I gave myself permission to ask for help and, more importantly, to receive it. It had been over two years since I had been part of a company, and emotionally, I didn't have much left to give. But I knew the basics, and I was exceptionally good at repeating them, over and over again.

Coach's Notes: Robin's decision to re-enter the industry with a fresh perspective is a powerful reminder that it's never too late to start again. Reinvention is always an option.

When grief would creep in and threaten to take me out, I leaned heavily on my support system—my business partners, who are now and will always be lifelong friends. Sometimes the weight of it all took me out for weeks, other times I couldn't function for over a month. But each time that happened, I stayed the course, applying the basics we all know and relying on the newfound love and support I had around me.

They may never fully understand how much they helped me or what they truly did for me, but they have my eternal gratitude. Forever in my heart, I will be grateful.

Understand this:

1. You are not what happened to you, despite how unfair, devastating, or tragic the event or events were.

2. You cannot let what you went through—or are going through—be for nothing.

3. If you've experienced the death of a child, partner, or any loved one, you cannot let their death be in vain.

4. You have to understand that you are not in this industry by accident! It's not a coincidence, and it's certainly not just to make a buck.

For those of you who have suffered and endured the worst of the worst, you are here to make a dent in the universe. Your journey, experiences, past, and tragedies—everything that makes you who you are—is meant to help those who don't yet have a voice and haven't found their way. Do you understand the magnitude of who you can reach, meet, and connect with through MLM? Do you realize how far your reach is? You are magic, my friend—pure f*cking magic!

So, it's okay! Sit in your anger, cry rivers of tears, isolate yourself if that's what you need, but DO NOT live there forever! You are needed! You are valued! You are so deeply loved! And if no one else tells you that, remember reading these words for the rest of your life.

Life is about living both tragically and magically at the same time. No matter what happens, always believe in the magic you hold within you. It's your greatest gift!

Remember when I said, I didn't always do things right. I burned bridges, tore down my own empires, and severed ties with people who loved me and helped me achieve my dreams. At one point, I was ready to turn my back on this entire industry, leaving nothing but destruction in my wake. I thought I was speaking the truth, but I was only causing harm.

But here's what I want you to know: My life has turned out better than I could have ever imagined. Not only have I found more success than I ever thought possible in this industry, but I also ended up marrying the man of my dreams. A man who lets me be my chaotic, hot mess, successful self. He gives me something I've never truly felt before—safety. Not just physical safety, but emotional safety, and for me, that is the greatest gift anyone could give.

My life shifted because I learned to live both tragically and magically at the same time. Despite my hard times, I still manage to have the capability to see opportunities, or what I call magic, present to me and I act on it!

CONCLUSION

Congratulations!

You just read an amazing book and I'm sure you've learned a lot. *But now what?!*

Did you just read that book for entertainment or you picked up this book because you wanted to make money?

If you're like many people, including myself, you grew up and heard this phrase that "knowledge is power." That's not true though.

Knowledge alone is NOT power. It's *applied knowledge* that is power, and that is especially true in business.

Why are so many network marketers stuck in their business even though they read books, attend events and go through a lot of personal development?!

The reason is because they don't know the difference between **Personal Development** versus **Personal Growth**. Personal Development is reading a book, listening to a podcast, attending a training, etc., **Personal Growth is when you actually** *take action* on something you've learned.

Some of the most well read network marketers that I know of don't make much money because they read and do personal development simply for *entertainment.*

They never take action! But I'm sure you're not the same way. You want to implement and make money. One important lesson I learned is that ***money loves speed!*** The faster you can implement what you just learned, the more money you will make! So how do you implement all these great nuggets that you just learned?

Many people get overwhelmed because they implement too many things all at once and never get good at anything. It's like going to the buffet and you see these great dishes and don't know where to start!

You end up eating everything but you don't really enjoy any specific type of dish because you never allow yourself to really savor what you eat before you move onto the next thing you stuff into your mouth! *The lack of focus also prevents consistency.* So here is how you can prevent overwhelm. The key is to focus on learning one thing at a time!

Take your favorite chapter and if you don't have one, then just choose one that you remember the most or the leader that resonated the most. If you still don't have one, then just pick any random chapter!

Go through that chapter again and then find one thing that you can implement right away, and then just start taking action!

You can apply the seven components of my **Consistency System** to make sure you take consistent action on that one thing you learned.

Here are the **7 Components of my Consistency System**

Component 1: Checklist
You must know exactly what you need to do

Component 2: Create and Schedule the Time
How will you have the time to work on the checklist?
When will you take action each day?
Ideally, you should schedule the same time each day.

Component 3: Determine the Strategy
How will you work on each step of the checklist?

Component 4: Choose Your Environment
Where will you take action?

Component 5: Tracking
How will you measure your progress and know if you're on track?

Component 6: Your Consistency Toolbox
What tools will you be using that'll help you be more efficient with your action steps?

Component 7: Accountability
Who is going to make sure you stay focused and consistent?

Once you successfully take action on the one thing, make sure you've added that to your daily routine before you move onto something else.

Never try to take action on more than one thing at a time because it just creates overwhelm and you never get good at anything.

So now it's your turn. Make sure you decide on what that one thing you will take action on and get going!

And remember...Consistency Creates Mastery!

Simon Chan
Consistency Coach, Podcaster, Speaker, Best Selling Author
Found of MLM Nation

www.ingramcontent.com/pod-product-compliance
Ingram Content Group UK Ltd.
Pitfield, Milton Keynes, MK11 3LW, UK
UKHW021843120125
453503UK00010B/152

9 798990 398856